Absolute Expert
DOLPHINS

All the
LATEST
FACTS From
the Field

Jennifer Swanson

With National Geographic Explorer
Justine Jackson-Ricketts

NATIONAL GEOGRAPHIC
Washington, D.C.

CONTENTS

CHAPTER 2
Dolphins: Inside and Out 32

CHAPTER 1
Meet the Dolphins 8

CHAPTER 3

A Dolphin's World 58

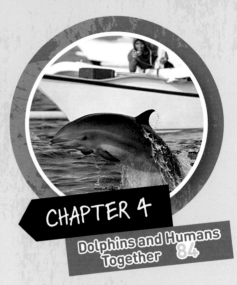

CHAPTER 4

Dolphins and Humans
Together 84

JUSTINE
JACKSON-RICKETTS

IRRAWADDY DOLPHIN
PALS JUMP INTO THE AIR.

FOREWORD

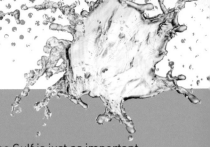

Hi! I'm Justine Jackson-Ricketts. I'm a marine biologist. I love dolphins! Dolphins are some of the most intelligent aquatic creatures on the planet, and they know how to have fun! They swim, jump, dive, and play with each other as they move through the ocean in groups called pods. With their enigmatic smiles, dolphins are the charmers of the undersea world.

I study Irrawaddy dolphins in particular. They are a small species of mammal found throughout southeast Asia and are considered to be at risk of becoming endangered. I study a population that lives in the Gulf of Thailand. My research involves "community ecology." That's learning how animals and plants interact with each other and their environments. Basically, I want to know where these dolphins live and what they eat.

I first take a look at their diet. One way I do that is to analyze stranded dolphins, ones that have washed up on shore. I take samples of their skin and teeth to perform experiments that will tell me what types of chemicals are present. The types of chemicals tell me what kind of food the dolphins have eaten. By observing where dolphin pods hang out and what the conditions are like there (temperature and depth, for example), I can start to make a map of their habitat.

There's something else I need to know in order to help save these dolphins: how they interact with people. Humans live around and use the Gulf of Thailand, too. They have for hundreds of years.

They fish and travel. The Gulf is just as important to their lives as it is for the dolphins'! So, we need to have a better understanding of how humans and dolphins overlap and interact in the Gulf.

In order to understand the dolphin–human interaction points, I created a map of where humans go in the Gulf. When I compare the human activity map with the dolphin habitat map, I look for how high human-use areas affect the dolphins' habitat and where these areas overlap. Do dolphins tend to live and eat near where there are a lot of boats (possibly an easy source of food!), or do the dolphins try to avoid humans? Does a lot of boat activity destroy the dolphins' habitat and decrease their population? Knowing these answers can help. They can aid local governments in making decisions about where boats can and cannot go. Perhaps the governments will set up laws to reduce the number of ships or boats in the area. Or maybe they will protect the dolphins' habitat and make it off-limits for human use. In any case, just knowing more about these incredible creatures makes other people curious about them, too!

All of these benefits can help Irrawaddy dolphins thrive. That's my goal as a marine biologist: to learn all that I can to protect aquatic species and also give back to the organisms we study. I want to make a difference for these animals. Don't you? So look for me throughout the book as we explore the seas and learn more about dolphins!

—Justine Jackson-Ricketts

SAY HELLO TO THE
BOTTLENOSE DOLPHIN!

CHAPTER 1
MEET THE DOLPHINS

INTRODUCTION

WHY DID I CHOOSE TO STUDY DOLPHINS?

I grew up in a corner of rural, mountainous Virginia, U.S.A. Tree-covered land with little water in sight. The ocean was like a far-off, fascinating country to me.

JUSTINE JACKSON-RICKETTS

I devoured books and nature programs about dolphins—those playful and intelligent creatures that inhabited an ocean realm so different from my backyard's green peaks and valleys.

The first time I saw dolphins up close was on a family trip to SeaWorld. We visited with some of the dolphins backstage. It was a magical experience. I knew I needed to learn more.

During high school, I attended a summer program in marine science at the University of Miami, where I learned about geology, marine environments, and coral identification. I even tried my hand at a small research project on fish. In college, I took all the life-science-related courses I could. Then the summer after my freshman year, I got a chance to study dolphins in their natural habitat. During an internship as a field assistant, I spent my days out on the ocean, observing bottlenose dolphins in the Florida Keys. It was even more exciting than seeing them backstage! Here I was, in the dolphins' own watery world, learning all I could about their behavior in the wild.

After that experience, I wanted to be a marine biologist more than anything. Being in the field also opened my eyes to different sea creatures. I began studying the ocean's ecosystem. My focus on dolphins drifted, as everyone and their cousin seemed to be studying them. I didn't see a niche for myself. But as it turned out, the dolphins weren't finished with me. I met the woman who would be my co-adviser at a conference. She was working on a project with Irrawaddy dolphins in Thailand and asked if I would be interested in researching their habitat. That little dolphin-obsessed five-year-old was still in me somewhere, and I couldn't say no.

FRIENDLY DOLPHIN STOPPING BY FOR A CLOSE-UP LOOK

I SPENT MY DAYS OUT ON THE OCEAN, LEARNING ALL I COULD ABOUT DOLPHINS' BEHAVIOR IN THE WILD.

DOLPHIN POD PERFORMING AT AN OCEANARIUM AND MARINE MAMMAL PARK

DOLPHINS ARE CREATURES THAT SPEND THEIR ENTIRE LIVES IN THE WATER.

They have fins and very strong tails. Sounds like they're fish, right? But they're not!

Dolphins are mammals, just like us. A mammal is an animal with special traits. First, mammals are warm-blooded. Warm-blooded animals are able to regulate their own body temperature. Humans can do that through sweating. Dolphins don't have sweat glands, so they regulate their body temperature another way. Dolphins have blubber, or extra layers of fat, to keep them warm in the cold ocean water.

Mammals are also vertebrates, which means that they have a backbone. A dolphin's strong backbone supports its body weight and skull. It is also flexible, allowing the dolphin to move its tail up and down easily during swimming. Fish swim by bending their tails from side to side, but dolphins' up-and-down motion shifts a lot of water in one big, strong stroke, helping them zoom through the ocean much faster than fish can.

Mammals also have hair on their bodies. Wait a minute. Dolphins don't have hair! If you've ever seen a dolphin, you know they have sleek, smooth bodies that glide through the water. When you touch them, they feel soft and slippery. However, dolphins are mammals, and so every single one of the more than 40 species of dolphins has hair.

That doesn't mean that dolphins have hair for their whole lives, though. While they are still developing, baby dolphins grow tiny whiskers around their noses. After they are born, the whiskers remain for a short time. Eventually, the tension of the water as they swim through it pulls the whiskers out. They never regrow. If you happen to look very closely at a dolphin, you may just see the tiny holes where its whiskers once grew.

CLOSE-UP OF THE VIBRISSAL CRYPTS, TINY PORES THAT HOLD THE WHISKERS

ELECTRIFYING WHISKERS

DOLPHINS MAY LOSE THEIR WHISKERS when they are young, but what's left behind is not just an empty hole. The holes are called vibrissal crypts. These specialized pores are small openings, similar to the ones that humans have in their skin. Unlike humans, however, the vibrissal crypts in a dolphin can sense electric fields. That's right. They can "feel" tiny electric pulses given off by other organisms. Scientists think this ability is used to find prey. How is this possible? The bottoms of the pores have nerve endings with a special mix of proteins and cells that sense electrical pulses. This signal goes to the dolphin's brain and lets it know that an animal is there. Dolphins are also known to use echolocation, or the ability to bounce sound off of objects to get the object's location. But these mammals are the first known to use electroreception, or the sensing of electric fields. That's especially helpful in very murky, or cloudy, waters, where it would be difficult to see and hear prey.

Fish breathe through their gills, tiny slits in their sides where oxygen from the water enters their bodies. But dolphins breathe air, just like humans do. They have a hole on top of their head, called a blowhole, that takes in oxygen from the air when the dolphin comes to the water's surface.

Fish lay eggs, but dolphins, like all mammals, give birth to their young and nurse them with milk that they produce. Baby dolphins, or calves, are unable to take care of themselves at first and require their mothers to watch over them. Dolphin calves typically stay with their mothers until they are between three and six years of age. The mothers teach them how to catch their food, avoid dangers, and navigate their habitat. When they have matured, they leave their mothers to join other juvenile, or "teenage," dolphins.

All in the Family

Dolphins belong to a class of mammals called cetaceans. Cetaceans are marine mammals, which means they are mammals that live in the water. There are more than 90 different types of cetaceans known to exist. These include all dolphins, whales, and porpoises living in oceans, rivers, and lakes. Cetaceans have been on Earth for millions of years, but they didn't always look like they do today. In fact, scientists believe that ancient ancestors of whales and dolphins actually had legs and walked on land! Today's whales and dolphins are distantly related to hoofed animals such as deer. How could a giant blue whale be related to a small forest-dwelling deer?

Fifty million years ago, the ancestor of both whales and dolphins was an animal the size of a raccoon called an *Indohyus*. Despite its small size, fossils of the *Indohyus* show that its legs and arms had a thick outer layer. Its bones were

SEE THE BUBBLE? DOLPHINS BREATHE THROUGH THE BLOWHOLE ON THE TOP OF THEIR HEAD.

HAS BLOWHOLE TO BREATHE
GIVES BIRTH TO YOUNG
FLEXES TAIL UP AND DOWN TO SWIM
HAS BLUBBER

DOLPHIN vs. FISH

HAS GILLS TO BREATHE
LAYS EGGS
BENDS TAIL SIDE TO SIDE TO SWIM
HAS SCALES

FISH, LIKE THE RAINBOW TROUT, BREATHE THROUGH GILLS ON THE SIDES OF THEIR HEAD.

heavy, allowing the animal to sink in the water instead of float. That would have been helpful for *Indohyus* to escape its predators. This same structure is found in the bones of whales and dolphins today. Scientists also believe that *Indohyus* was an aquatic animal because the chemicals in its teeth show that it swallowed water as it ate.

Next came *Pakicetus*. Like *Indohyus*, *Pakicetus* were small hoofed animals, about the size of a wolf, that walked on land. Yet scientists call *Pakicetus* the "first whale." Unlike *Indohyus*, which were herbivores, *Pakicetus* had long skulls and were carnivores. They likely ate meat the way modern whales do. Scientists also discovered a direct link from the *Pakicetus* fossils to today's whales: *Pakicetus* has an ear bone with a unique feature that today is known to exist only in whales.

So how did the ancestors of whales and dolphins go from hooves to fins? Over time, the descendants of

Pakicetus spent more time in the water, both in freshwater and salt water. Their bodies adapted by growing shorter, wider legs that could be used as paddles. Their bodies also grew longer, and tails appeared. Eventually, in later descendants such as the *Basilosaurus*, these legs disappeared completely and were replaced with flippers.

Basilosaurus, which means "king lizard," lived between 40 and 34 million years ago. These ancient whales were 40 to 65 feet (12–20 m) long and were the largest known animal at the time. They may have lived exclusively in water, because they had tailfins and backbones like modern whales. Basilosaurids had extremely small hind legs that may have actually been inside their body. These legs were most likely left over as generations moved from land to the sea. In fact, some modern whales are occasionally found to have tiny, rod-shaped bones next to their

BASILOSAURUS IS A MARINE MAMMAL THAT LIVED IN THE CENOZOIC PERIOD—THE AGE OF MAMMALS.

THE SKULL OF A *PAKICETUS*, THE FIRST WHALE

A DORUDON, WHICH LIVED MORE THAN 34 MILLION YEARS AGO

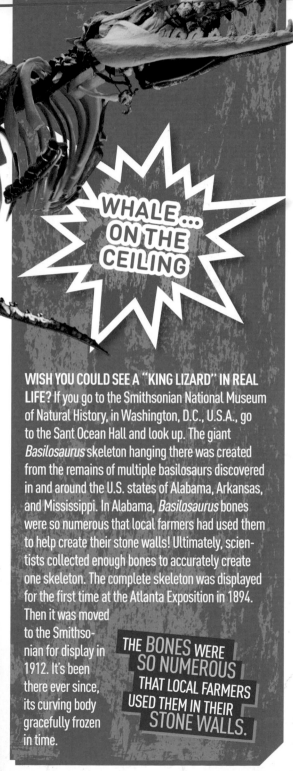

pelvis. These are believed to be the same hind legs found in their ancestors.

After *Basilosaurus* came the two groups of whales that include the modern whales: the *Mysticeti* (baleen whales) and the *Odontoceti* (toothed whales). All of these whales are part of the cetacean family.

Calling All Cetaceans

Scientists separate the cetaceans into two different groups: toothed whales and baleen whales. Dolphins and porpoises are in the toothed whale group, along with orcas, sperm whales, beaked whales, belugas, narwhals, and freshwater dolphins. The toothed whales have more than 73 species of animals. The baleen whale group consists of 11 different species of whales, including the pygmy right whale and the blue whale. When it comes to whales versus dolphins just remember: All dolphins are whales, but not all whales are dolphins.

AMBULOCETUS, WHICH LIVED MORE THAN 50 MILLION YEARS AGO

WHALE... ON THE CEILING

WISH YOU COULD SEE A "KING LIZARD" IN REAL LIFE? If you go to the Smithsonian National Museum of Natural History, in Washington, D.C., U.S.A., go to the Sant Ocean Hall and look up. The giant *Basilosaurus* skeleton hanging there was created from the remains of multiple basilosaurs discovered in and around the U.S. states of Alabama, Arkansas, and Mississippi. In Alabama, *Basilosaurus* bones were so numerous that local farmers had used them to help create their stone walls! Ultimately, scientists collected enough bones to accurately create one skeleton. The complete skeleton was displayed for the first time at the Atlanta Exposition in 1894. Then it was moved to the Smithsonian for display in 1912. It's been there ever since, its curving body gracefully frozen in time.

THE BONES WERE SO NUMEROUS THAT LOCAL FARMERS USED THEM IN THEIR STONE WALLS.

FAMILY TREE

ALL LIVING THINGS ARE BROKEN DOWN INTO BIG GROUPS. Then, each group is broken down into smaller and smaller groups, based on how the living things are alike. Where do dolphins fit in their family tree? Here's where the common bottlenose dolphin sits:

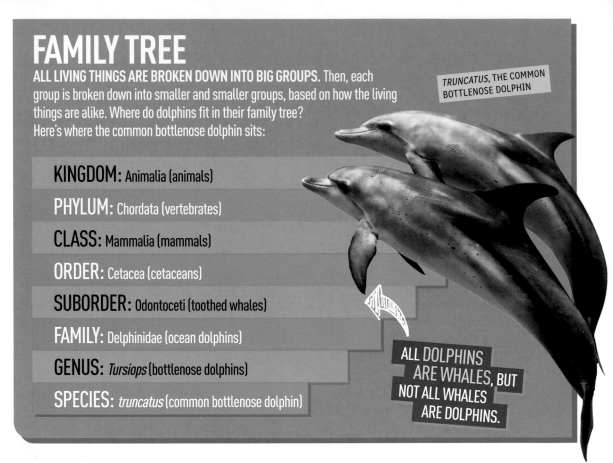

TRUNCATUS, THE COMMON BOTTLENOSE DOLPHIN

KINGDOM: Animalia (animals)

PHYLUM: Chordata (vertebrates)

CLASS: Mammalia (mammals)

ORDER: Cetacea (cetaceans)

SUBORDER: Odontoceti (toothed whales)

FAMILY: Delphinidae (ocean dolphins)

GENUS: *Tursiops* (bottlenose dolphins)

SPECIES: *truncatus* (common bottlenose dolphin)

ALL DOLPHINS ARE WHALES, BUT NOT ALL WHALES ARE DOLPHINS.

Have Teeth? Join the Pod

You can tell the difference between toothed whales and baleen whales without looking in their mouths. Toothed whales have one blowhole on top of their head, and baleen whales have two. Toothed whales have teeth, though they use them for capturing, not chewing, their prey. Baleen whales do not have teeth, but rather plates, which are flexible and made of a material called keratin. Keratin is the same material that makes up human fingernails.

AN ORCA, OR KILLER WHALE, IS ALSO A DOLPHIN.

Baleen whales eat by sucking tiny fish or plankton (microscopic animals and plants) into their mouth and filtering out the water through the plates. The plates act as a barrier: The food stays in, and the water goes out.

Toothed whales use their teeth to capture their prey, but they don't actually use their teeth for chewing. Instead, they swallow their food whole. Toothed whales are quite social and like to live in groups, called pods. Pods can range in size from 2 to 40 members. Larger "super pods" containing up to 1,000 members

SPERM WHALES ARE THE LARGEST OF THE TOOTHED WHALES.

have been spotted. These large groups can even contain more than one species of dolphin or porpoise. The pods are usually a mix of males and females but can be only females and their young, or even all males, on occasion. For toothed whales, the males tend to grow larger than the females. Toothed whales use echolocation, or the bouncing of sound off of objects, to navigate. Some species may even use electroreception—the ability to detect electrical currents from a moving animal like a fish—to spot their prey.

Whales With Plates Stand Alone

Baleen whales make up a smaller group of cetaceans. With only around 11 species of them in the ocean, they are much less populous than toothed whales. Baleen whales are larger than toothed whales and include the fin whale, the humpback whale, and the blue whale, the largest animal on Earth. Despite their size, baleen whales are harder to find in the wild than toothed whales. Why? Because they are usually

only seen by humans when they are surfacing for air. That is less than 20 percent of the time they are swimming. So more than 80 percent of the time, baleen whales are underwater.

Unlike toothed whales, which like to travel in pods, baleen whales mostly swim by themselves or in small groups for short periods of time. Groups form only during reproduction or migration. The males tend to be smaller than the females. The bond between a mother baleen whale and her calf is very strong. Calves stay with their mothers for up to a year feeding and learning how to survive. Much of the behavior of these amazing animals is still unknown since it is difficult for scientists to find them underwater and track their movements.

BALEEN WHALES HAVE PLATES, NOT TEETH, IN THEIR GIANT MOUTHS.

AN AMAZON RIVER DOLPHIN IS EASILY RECOGNIZABLE BY ITS PINK COLOR.

INDO-PACIFIC HUMPBACK DOLPHINS LEAP IN TANDEM NEAR HONG KONG, CHINA.

Species of Dolphin

Even though dolphins are a part of the toothed whale group, they are their own family. When you say "dolphin," many people instantly picture a bottlenose dolphin. Why? You can find them in most aquarium and aquatic shows. You can tell a bottlenose dolphin by its long, sleek body, small fin, and strong tail. Their curvy mouth and big eyes give them the look of a permanent smile. Makes you want to smile right back at them. But bottlenose dolphins aren't the only type of dolphins in the world. There are more than 37 different species of oceanic dolphins in the Delphinidae family. Members range in size from the tiny Guiana dolphin to giant orcas. There are seven species of river dolphins in three different families that live in freshwater rivers or estuaries. The exact number of dolphin species changes, because occasionally new species are discovered.

PINK DOLPHINS, LIKE THIS ONE, ARE USUALLY FOUND IN RIVERS.

River Dolphins

River dolphins live almost exclusively in freshwater rivers and estuaries, partially enclosed bodies of water near the coast. Many are found in and around the rivers of South America and Asia, including the Amazon, Ganges, Indus, Yangtze, and Mekong. The seven species of river dolphins tend to be smaller than their ocean-dwelling cousins, as they reach only about eight feet (2.4 m) when they are fully grown. Just like ocean dolphins, however, river dolphins can be brown, gray, or black. Indo-Pacific humpback dolphins and Amazon river dolphins are pink. River dolphins tend to live in highly populated areas, which means they have a lot of interaction with humans. Getting caught in fishing nets, hit by boat traffic, and swimming in polluted waters are just a few dangers that affect a river dolphin's life. Because of this constantly changing environment, many river dolphins are highly susceptible to becoming extinct. Dolphin numbers, particularly in and around Asia, have dwindled to alarmingly low rates.

POROISES, LIKE THIS HARBOR PORPOISE FOUND OFF THE COAST OF NORWAY, SPORT A SHORTER, SMALLER "GRIN."

Porpoise Cousins

Porpoises are like a kind of cousin to the dolphin. They are in the same Delphinidae family, but porpoises look different from a typical dolphin. A dolphin has a larger forehead and a long beak, or nose. A porpoise has a smaller head with no beak. Its nose is smaller and rounder. A porpoise's mouth is smaller than a dolphin's. Its teeth are square, while a dolphin's are pointy. The triangular dorsal fin of a porpoise is also smaller and located in the middle of its back. Porpoises are quiet compared to the talkative dolphins. They don't make the same whistling noises with their blowhole that dolphins do. There are only six species of porpoises, which means there are a lot fewer porpoises in the world than dolphins. But both of these highly intelligent aquatic creatures sport that same trademark grin.

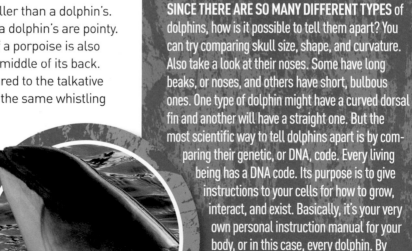

SMILE! THIS PORPOISE GRINS BIG.

WHO'S WHO?

SINCE THERE ARE SO MANY DIFFERENT TYPES of dolphins, how is it possible to tell them apart? You can try comparing skull size, shape, and curvature. Also take a look at their noses. Some have long beaks, or noses, and others have short, bulbous ones. One type of dolphin might have a curved dorsal fin and another will have a straight one. But the most scientific way to tell dolphins apart is by comparing their genetic, or DNA, code. Every living being has a DNA code. Its purpose is to give instructions to your cells for how to grow, interact, and exist. Basically, it's your very own personal instruction manual for your body, or in this case, every dolphin. By studying the DNA code of each dolphin, scientists are able to determine any slight changes that might exist between two dolphins. These changes mean that these two dolphins are of different species.

MEET THE IRRAWADDY DOLPHIN

THIS IRRAWADDY DOLPHIN MAKES A RARE APPEARANCE ABOVE THE WATER.

WITH THEIR LARGE, ROUND HEADS and little to no nose, Irrawaddy dolphins look more like beluga whales than dolphins. Despite their appearance, scientists believe Irrawaddy dolphins are probably closely related to orcas. An Irrawaddy dolphin can weigh between 198 and 440 pounds (90–200 kg), and males are heavier than females. They are typically shorter than bottlenose dolphins at six to nine feet (1.8–2.7 m) long. Irrawaddy dolphins are dark gray or dark blue and have a lighter gray body underneath. They have long, wide flippers and a short dorsal, or top, fin.

Irrawaddy dolphins are found in the coastal regions of South and Southeast Asia and in rivers located in these areas. They live in marine (saltwater) or freshwater rivers and estuaries. These dolphins are considered to be highly vulnerable; fewer than 7,000 of them are known to exist.

These wonderful animals are shy and will not approach humans. They are hard to spot because they can dive deep and come up to breathe only every one to three minutes. When they do surface, you have to look quickly. Only their head pops up and they take a quick breath before diving again. It is rare to see them flip their tail or jump out of the water like other dolphins. They can hold their breath as long as 12 minutes.

Irrawaddy dolphins feed on fish, cephalopods, and crustaceans. They tend to travel in small pods of three to six dolphins, although pods as large as 30 have been spotted. The biggest threat to Irrawaddy dolphins is humans. The dolphins are captured for food or accidentally caught in fishing nets, and their habitats are being destroyed by increased boating traffic, mining, dam construction, and deforestation of mangroves.

FEWER THAN 7,000 IRRAWADDY DOLPHINS ARE KNOWN TO EXIST.

NOTICE THE SHORT DORSAL FIN ON THE IRRAWADDY DOLPHIN.

SHORT DORSAL FIN

SHORT ROSTRUM

A Whale of a Relation

Both pilot whales and orcas are in the Delphinidae family. That means that they're dolphins. Surprised? Many people are. After all, an orca can weigh as much as 12,000 pounds (5,440 kg) and be more than 30 feet (9 m) long. That's really big! Despite their immense size, orcas are some of the fastest animals in the ocean. They can swim up to 30 miles an hour (48 km/h). Some people call orcas "killer" whales. That's because they eat other dolphins and small whales. It is not because they eat or attack humans. In fact, there's no known instance of an orca in the wild ever attacking a human. The orcas try to avoid humans if they encounter them, by swimming off and diving deep.

Pilot whales are slightly smaller than orcas but still very large compared to other dolphins.

A SHORT-FINNED PILOT WHALE BREACHES.

They have rounded heads and snouts, or noses, and are usually all black or very dark gray in color. They range in length from 16 to 20 feet (4.9–6.1 m) and can weigh from 1.5 to 3 tons (1.4–2.7 t). Pilot whales, like all dolphins, are extremely intelligent. One pilot whale in captivity was trained by U.S. Navy scientists to recover small objects from the ocean floor. The pilot whale, named Morgan, used his sonar to locate a tiny beeper and then carried it in his mouth to another drop-off point. Talk about a great retriever! Not even your dog could dive to a depth of 1,600 feet (488 m). Pilot whales are very sociable animals and usually swim in pods of 20 to 90. These gigantic creatures stay together, even when stranding, or beaching, themselves on the shore. Scientists don't know why pilot whales do this, and they are working to understand and prevent this phenomenon.

DID YOU KNOW?

- **AT BIRTH, AN ORCA** weighs up to 400 pounds (181 kg) and is about eight feet (2.4 m) long. Talk about a big baby!
- **ORCAS CANNOT SMELL.** Why? No nose! In fact, they don't even have a part of their brain that can process smells. Instead, they rely on sight and hearing.
- **ORCAS, LIKE DOLPHINS, CAN SLEEP** with one eye open. This allows them to let one half of their brain sleep while the other half stays awake and alert.

AN ORCA COMING TO THE SURFACE FOR AIR

WHERE TO FIND DOLPHINS

DOLPHINS AND WHALES CAN BE FOUND in practically every body of water all across the planet. From as far north as the Arctic Ocean, through the warm, tropical waters near the Equator, to the cold Antarctic, you will see dolphins. No one dolphin goes to all of these places. Each species has their own habitat or range where they are comfortable. Some are found only in marine or ocean waters. Others live only in freshwater estuaries and rivers. Irrawaddy dolphins, finless porpoises, and the tucuxi can live in both marine water and freshwater.

RISSO'S DOLPHINS are mostly found off the coast of California near Monterey Bay, and in northern waters near British Columbia. They are some of the largest dolphin species and like the warmer waters, tending to avoid the cold waters to the north.

ARCTIC

NORTH AMERICA

PACIFIC OCEAN

Monterey Bay

The **INDO-PACIFIC HUMPBACK DOLPHIN** likes the warm, tropical waters of the Indian and Pacific Oceans. They swim close to shore and enjoy hanging out near coral reefs and mangrove forests.

BOTTLENOSE DOLPHINS are found in tropical oceans and other warm waters around the globe. Basically, they can be found in every ocean of the world except the Arctic.

PACIFIC OCEAN

INDIAN OCEAN

AUSTRALIA

HECTOR'S DOLPHIN is a smaller dolphin that swims in and around the waters of New Zealand. They like shallow, coastal waters; estuaries; and areas around the mouth of a river.

OCEAN

MAP KEY
- ☐ Polar waters
- ☐ Temperate waters
- ☐ Tropical and subtropical waters

ORCAS are found in every ocean in the world, but they particularly like the colder regions. They are most often seen in the Pacific Northwest, along northern Norway's coast in the Atlantic, and in the waters surrounding Antarctica.

EUROPE

ASIA

Mediterranean Sea

Gulf of Mexico

ATLANTIC OCEAN

Caribbean Sea

The **PINK DOLPHIN** lives in the warm waters of the Amazon River. It likes the shallow, fast-flowing, white-water rivers, either clear or black (cloudy).

AFRICA

Amazon River

IRRAWADDY DOLPHINS enjoy swimming along the coasts of Southeast Asia. They prefer the muddy waters near the mouths of rivers in India, Thailand, Cambodia, and Bangladesh.

SOUTH AMERICA

ATLANTIC OCEAN

INDIAN OCEAN

STRIPED DOLPHINS are found in warm, tropical seas pretty much all around the world. Specifically, they are seen both near the coastal regions and out in the offshore regions in the Mediterranean Sea, the Pacific Ocean, the Atlantic Ocean, the Indian Ocean, and the Caribbean Sea, and in the northern Gulf of Mexico.

ANTARCTICA

NO-SWIMMING AREAS WITH SPINNER DOLPHINS

SPINNER DOLPHINS ARE SOME OF THE FRIENDLIEST DOLPHINS AROUND. They are very social and quite curious about the world around them. They love to jump, dive, swim, and even do flips. Spinner dolphins are found off the coast of Hawaii, U.S.A. These small, slender dolphins are about six to seven feet (1.8–2 m) long and can weigh from 130 to 170 pounds (59–77 kg). During the day, spinner dolphins love to spend time swimming and frolicking in the deep depths of the ocean. At night, they love to rest near the coves and inlets of the islands. People have figured out that they can get an up-close look at these amazing creatures then, and scientists worry that this is causing behavior changes in the dolphins because they are not getting the rest they need. In addition, sometimes the constant contact with humans makes the dolphins move to a new cove. There they may find predators, so the number of spinner dolphins is declining in Hawaii. New laws have been put into place to keep humans from interfering with the dolphins. After all, they need their sleep. How would you like your sleep disturbed every night? Might make you kind of cranky. No one wants a cranky dolphin.

A POD OF SPINNER DOLPHINS SWIMS NEAR THE BIG ISLAND, HAWAII.

At Home With Dolphins

A habitat is where dolphins swim, eat, reproduce, and live together as a pod. Many times dolphins must migrate, or travel from one place to another, to find the best habitat. Migration is a huge part of a dolphin's life. Sometimes they migrate to find warmer waters when the temperatures drop during fall and winter. For example, the Atlantic bottlenose dolphin's habitat ranges from Cape Cod, Massachusetts, to the coast of Virginia. These dolphins swim north in the spring when the waters are warmer off the shores of Massachusetts, and they swim south in the fall. Why travel so far? It's not just for the warm waters—it's also to eat! Bottlenose dolphins migrate to follow the fish, squid, and crustaceans that are their food source. Dolphins will stay in a certain area as long as the food is plentiful and the waters are warm. Quite naturally,

they also like places where the predators, or animals that might use them as a food source, are scarce.

Dolphins don't have many predators in the ocean. Why not? Dolphins are a bit difficult to catch. Only the stronger, larger sharks or orcas even try to eat them. In the presence of predators, dolphins form a circle around the weaker ones in the pod. They violently attack any predator that comes near.

With few predators, you would think that dolphins are free to go wherever they want in the oceans and rivers. Not always. Some of the biggest dangers to dolphins and their habitats are caused by humans. These include when boat and ship traffic increases, when the food source for dolphins is reduced through overfishing or pollution, and even when dolphins are captured by humans for consumption. Climate change is also beginning to have an effect on dolphin habitats. As worldwide temperatures rise, the ocean gets warmer or cooler in certain areas. Drastic temperature changes will make dolphins seek new, milder habitats. Some areas in the ocean that were once home to huge pods of dolphins are now quite empty. Why does this happen? Dolphins are very smart. They won't return to areas where the habitat is too polluted or there isn't enough food for them to survive. The disappearance of dolphin habitats is concerning, and it has resulted in many places being declared as protected areas or sanctuaries for these marine animals. Boats, ships, fishing, and even pollution are greatly reduced or completely eliminated in these areas to keep them clean for the dolphins.

Intelligent Creatures of the Deep

Dolphins are extremely intelligent animals. They appear to have complex relationships, can perform difficult tasks, and seem to remember many different things at once. It is thought that dolphins are one of the rare animals to possess problem-solving abilities similar to humans. These traits make them fascinating subjects for study and learning. To discover how smart dolphins really are, researchers have designed games for captive dolphins and watch to see how they perform. In one study, a dolphin needed to indicate that it understood "less" versus "more." First they presented the dolphin with two black boards. Each board had a different number of white dots affixed to it. The dolphin was trained to indicate which board had fewer dots. This study showed that dolphins understand math. In another research program, dolphins were trained to understand object permanence. An object, such as a ball, was presented to them. Then it was hidden behind a board. They learned to understand that the ball was still there, behind the board, even though they couldn't see it.

Learning how dolphins behave in captivity and in the wild is also important. If we can understand their habitats, what they need to survive, and how they work together in their pods, we can get an idea of how their society is structured. Why is it important to understand this? If we can figure out how dolphins behave within their environment, it might teach us more about their interactions with other marine animals. It would also help us determine where dolphins fit in the marine ecosystem and how important they are to other species and to our planet as a whole.

THIS STUDY SHOWED THAT DOLPHINS UNDERSTAND MATH.

A TRAINER WORKS WITH A DOLPHIN IN A TRUE DOT STUDY.

BET YOU DIDN'T KNOW!

Dolphins don't drink water.
While they live in seawater, they never drink it. If they drink it, they get sick.

Dolphins have been around for millions of years.
Images of dolphins have been found in ancient cities from as early as 312 B.C. That's pretty old!

Dolphins can live to be 50 years old.
Their life expectancy depends on many factors, including environment, the amount of predators, and their food supply.

Dolphins don't use their teeth for eating.
Instead, they use them to capture their fish and swallow them whole. They don't even have jaw muscles for chewing, so they couldn't chew if they wanted to.

One tablespoon of water in a dolphin's lungs could cause it to drown.
Dolphins have lungs similar to humans'. If you were to get two tablespoons of water in your lungs, you could drown; a dolphin could drown with just one tablespoon.

Dolphins can stay awake for up to five days at a time.

Sleeping is difficult since they can't breathe while they sleep. When they do relax, they shut down half of their brain, and the other half keeps them breathing and aware of their surroundings.

Dolphins can recognize their own reflections in a mirror.

They are very intelligent. Not many animals have the ability to do this. The list includes: orangutans, chimpanzees, gorillas, elephants, orcas, bonobos, rhesus macaques, European magpies, and, of course, humans.

When a dolphin dives underwater, it is holding its breath.

Dolphins cannot breathe underwater. They need to surface to get air from the atmosphere. Good thing they can hold their breath for up to five to seven minutes.

The blowhole of a dolphin is actually a nose.

A dolphin's blowhole works just like a human nose, because it takes in and expels oxygen. Of course, it is on the top of the dolphin's head to make it easier for them to breathe when they surface.

Dolphins heal very fast.

They have the ability to regrow tissue, even if there is a lot of damage, very quickly.

FEEDING TIME! A DOLPHIN IS ON THE HUNT FOR ITS DINNER.

DIET STUDIES CAN LEAD TO CONSERVATION EFFORTS THAT HELP KEEP THE OCEANS HEALTHY AND CLEAN.

Keeping Our Oceans Healthy

Dolphins swim in every ocean on the planet. That makes them a great resource for information about the health of the marine environment. Researchers refer to dolphins as bioindicators, a living organism that measures the health of an ecosystem. Since dolphins don't have many predators, they are at the top of the food chain, so if the dolphins in a particular area are seen to be vibrant, active, and in large numbers, then there's a pretty good chance that the ocean in that area is a strong and beneficial environment. That means pollution is low, interference from ships and boats is minimal, and the water temperatures are just right.

Sick, injured, or dead dolphins can indicate that something is wrong with the ocean environment. For this reason, researchers like Justine keep a watchful eye on dolphin pods throughout the world. They study dolphins that have died in order to figure out if it was by natural causes or by an outside influence. Researchers will also capture sick dolphins in order to determine what types of diseases they might have and where they may have gotten them. This information is very valuable not just to dolphin researchers but also to ocean specialists and environmentalists. Through many studies, researchers have learned that if a dolphin has a disease in its immune system, it cannot reproduce normally, and that if it has cancer, it is most likely due to pollution in the water. The source of this pollution can then be tracked down and addressed. It might be from agricultural, residential, and industrial runoff, or even oil spills. The issues can be taken care of with proper disposal and eco-friendly efforts.

Dolphin studies are indicators of the health of other animals as well. Since many species of aquatic animals live within the same areas, if the dolphins aren't healthy, the other species probably aren't either. For example, a dolphin could die from eating a contaminated fish. That will lead researchers to ask how the fish became diseased. Where did it get infected? And also, do humans consume this type of fish, too? If so, researchers will be able to alert fishing boats and restaurants to stop capturing and serving these fish to humans. So learning all we can about dolphins can actually help us, too.

Interestingly enough, fish that might be harmful to humans might not be harmful to dolphins. Dolphins have been known to eat fish that contain the toxin ciguatera. Ciguatera is very harmful to humans if ingested. It can cause nausea, stomach pain, and even cardiac and neurological symptoms, such as vertigo, in humans. It is rarely life-threatening, but it can be very serious. When dolphins eat them, these fish are less likely to be caught by fishermen. One Peruvian ecology group refers to the dolphins as the "sanitary police of the ocean." In other words, dolphins help keep the ocean clean by reducing overall fish populations and by keeping dangerous fish off of our dinner plates!

Conservation

Dolphins are some of the most amazing marine animals on the planet. With their engaging "smiles," playful behavior, and extreme intelligence, they are fun and exciting to watch.

Humans can learn a lot from these awesome mammals of the deep. But we learn more than just about the animals themselves. Researchers study dolphins to determine the types of food they are eating. A change in diet can be a signal that something is wrong with the environment. Diet studies can lead to conservation efforts that help keep the oceans healthy and clean. Injured dolphins can also alert researchers to something unusual, or even illegal, that might be happening in an area. Dolphins that are killed by harpoons may mean that illegal fishing or hunting is taking place. (Dolphins are protected by the Marine Mammal Protection Act of 1972. Purposely injuring a dolphin or trying to capture one without the proper permit procedures is illegal.) People found participating in these activities are arrested and can be fined or imprisoned.

A DOLPHIN PLAYS WITH A BIT OF SEAWEED.

SNORKEL AND MASK NEEDED FOR DIVING

DEEP DIVE

DESIGN A DOLPHIN STUDY!

RESEARCHERS STUDY DOLPHINS for many different reasons. Some want to learn more about their intelligence, social interactions, and how they live and reproduce. Others want to know more about dolphin habitats and how they affect the ocean as a whole. Still other researchers are looking to dolphins for help with conservation and with reducing the human effect on the marine ecosystem.

What do you want to know about dolphins? What questions would you ask? How would you try to find the answers?

TAKING NOTES ON OBSERVATIONS IS IMPORTANT FOR RESEARCH.

My Dolphin Research

Questions I want to answer:

1. How deep can a dolphin dive?
2. What is a dolphin's favorite food?
3. Dolphins prefer living in warm water or cold water?

How will I get my answers

1. Gather existing data from online sources
2. Go to the library for relevant books
3. Contact a dolphin researcher or marine biologist

Dolphin statistics

Habitat: _____

Predators: _____

Prey: _____

A SHORT-BEAKED COMMON DOLPHIN LEAPS IN THE AIR BEFORE DIVING DEEP.

CHAPTER 2

DOLPHINS: INSIDE AND OUT

INTRODUCTION

BEING OUT IN THE FIELD IS AN INTERESTING EXPERIENCE,

but it's not always exciting. You are settled into a small boat for up to eight hours or so a day, continuously scanning open water for any sign of a dolphin.

JUSTINE JACKSON-RICKETTS

Binoculars can be helpful since they help you to see a long distance, but their tiny visual fields can make you miss something up close. So mostly you just use your own eyes to look around. The waves of the ocean rock the boat, and you may feel slightly off-center or even tired as they lull you to sleep, but you must keep watch! It is difficult to spot a fin above the water, because the Irrawaddy dolphins that we study have very small dorsal fins. We scan the water for disruptions in the waves, or perhaps the flip of a tail, if we are lucky.

Seeing a fin isn't the only tricky part. Within our area, we see three species of dolphins: the Irrawaddy, the Indo-Pacific humpback, and the Indo-Pacific finless porpoise. The Indo-Pacific humpback dolphins are easy to identify. They are pink! Irrawaddy dolphins and Indo-Pacific finless porpoises are both gray. But, as their name suggests, finless porpoises don't have a fin. So if we see a gray fin, it's an Irrawaddy!

As we keep scanning, someone shouts "Sighting!" We spring into action. Someone calls out the waypoint (the exact GPS position or latitude and longitude of our position). Another person calculates the distance to the dolphin, the angle of its approach to our craft (to make sure we don't run into it), and if it's a pod, how many dolphins there are. Using the environmental probe, we measure water temperature, the clarity of the water (how clear or cloudy it is), the state of the water (choppy with a lot of waves, or calm), its depth (how deep it is), and its pH and salinity (the levels of acidity and salt).

If we can see four different pods of dolphins in one day, that is a success. There are a lot of days when we see only one pod of dolphins, and there are days when we don't see any at all. The more we know and learn about their natural habitats, though, the more likely we are to have at least one sighting of Irrawaddy dolphins per day.

AN IRRAWADDY POKES ITS HEAD ABOVE THE WATER FOR A QUICK SMILE.

IT IS DIFFICULT TO SPOT A FIN ABOVE THE WATER, BECAUSE **IRRAWADDY DOLPHINS HAVE VERY SMALL DORSAL FINS.**

INDO-PACIFIC HUMPBACK DOLPHINS ARE EASY TO IDENTIFY. THEY ARE PINK!

AN INDO-PACIFIC HUMPBACK DOLPHIN BREACHES, OR LEAPS, INTO THE AIR.

WHEN YOU THINK OF THE **PERFECT MARINE MAMMAL,** DO YOU IMAGINE A **DOLPHIN?**

You should. Dolphins are built for swimming. With their sleek, streamlined bodies, flexible flippers and fins, and mighty tails, they are some of the oceans' fastest swimmers.

The orca can reach speeds of more than 34.5 miles an hour (55.5 km/h). Bottlenose dolphins clock in at a top speed of 23.6 miles an hour (38 km/h).

What makes dolphins so fast?

First, their body shape is naturally curved, which allows them to glide through the water with very little drag, or friction. Think of it this way. If you were to push a grapefruit through the water, you would have to push pretty hard. As you push on the grapefruit, you would feel the water pushing back at you. That is a force called drag. Now try pushing a banana through the water. The force pushing back at you—the drag—would be less. That is because the banana is smaller, more curved, and stream-lined. That shape disrupts less of the water and allows it to flow more easily around the sides of the banana. Why are we talking about fruit? A banana is shaped like a dolphin. So if a banana has less drag in the water, so will a dolphin.

Flex Your Pecs

A dolphin's sleek body is just one of the charac-teristics that make it a natural swimmer. Another is its fins. Every dolphin, whale, and porpoise has five fins that help it streak through the water at top speed.

Two of the most noticeable flippers are the pectoral fins. Pectoral means "front," which is where they are found on a dolphin's body—one

AN AMAZON RIVER DOLPHIN FLEXES ITS PECTORAL FINS ON A BREACH.

DOLPHINS HAVE A STREAMLINED HEAD SO THEY CAN CUT THROUGH THE WATER QUICKLY.

on each side. They help the dolphin stop, start, and steer underwater. While they are not used for propulsion (moving forward and faster), the pectoral fins, in combination with the dorsal fin, help with balance. Their steadying influence keeps the dolphin swimming straight and upright.

The pectoral fins are the only fins that contain bones. Inside these fins are bones similar to the ones found in a human arm and hand. Just like humans, dolphins have a humerus, which is like the upper part of your arm. They also have a radius and ulna, the two bones that make up your lower arm. They even have a ball and socket that attaches them, better known to you as your elbow. At the end of these "arm" bones are phalanges, or "fingers." Each finger is composed of a set of tiny bones, just like yours. Why are these there? It's not like the dolphin needs

BONES FOUND IN A DOLPHIN'S FLIPPER

hands or arms to swim. Flippers are much better for that. Scientists believe that these bones are left over from the time when dolphins lived on land and had arms and hands.

High-Top Calling Card

A dolphin's most visible fin is its dorsal fin. Dorsal means "back," which is where it is located on a dolphin, whale, or porpoise. Dorsal fins come in all shapes and sizes. Orcas have huge dorsal fins. A male orca can have a dorsal fin that reaches as high as six feet (1.8 m) into the air. That's a little bit taller than an average adult human male.

THE PECTORAL FINS ARE THE ONLY FINS THAT CONTAIN BONES.

AN ORCA'S PECTORAL FINS ARE SHAPED LIKE A PADDLE.

AN UP-CLOSE LOOK AT AN ATLANTIC SPOTTED DOLPHIN

BLOWHOLE
Dolphins breathe through a hole near the back of their head called a blowhole. Dolphins exhale and inhale extremely fast, taking a breath in a third of a second. Air blasts from the blowhole at 100 miles an hour (161 km/h).

MELON
This fatty, rounded section of a dolphin's forehead is called a melon. It's used to focus and transmit the sound waves produced for echolocation.

ROSTRUM
A dolphin's beak-like snout is called a rostrum.

TEETH
Dolphins swallow food whole, but they still have up to 250 pointy, cone-shaped teeth for grabbing fish.

EYES
A dolphin's eyeballs move independently of each other. For example, one eye can look straight ahead, while the other looks straight up. Try it! Not so easy, right?

DORSAL FIN

A dorsal fin helps dolphins stay balanced in the water. The height of the fin can vary widely. An orca's dorsal fin can be six feet (1.8 m) tall! Some species barely have one at all. Their fin looks more like a hump.

FLUKE

A powerful tail fin called a fluke propels dolphins through the water.

PEDUNCLE

The muscular ridge of the peduncle strengthens the tail, helping the dolphin swim fast and jump out of the water.

SKIN

A dolphin's smooth skin feels like rubber. Like our skin, a dolphin's is delicate and sensitive to the touch. It's kept smooth by constantly being rubbed off and replaced.

EARS

A dolphin's ear holes are easy to miss. They're about the size of a crayon tip. Yet dolphins have some of the best hearing in the animal kingdom.

PECTORAL FINS

Dolphins' pectoral fins, or flippers, are their steering mechanism, helping them start, stop, and turn.

PECTORAL
FINS

DORSAL
FIN

PEDUNCLE

FLUKE

A SMALL POD OF DOLPHINS
BREACHES HIGH INTO THE AIR.

Female orcas have smaller dorsal fins, at only three to four feet (0.9–1.2 m) tall. Most dolphins have dorsal fins that are curved and located in the middle of their back. Porpoises' dorsal fins are triangular and shorter. Some dolphins, like the finless porpoise, have small rounded humps that serve as their dorsal fin. Regardless of size, all dorsal fins are made of dense, fibrous, connective tissue. There are no bones, cartilage, or muscle inside. The tissue makes the fins strong but flexible, and, with the pectoral fins, allows the dorsal fin to act as a balancing mechanism for the swimming dolphin.

One of the most important functions of the dorsal fin is to regulate the dolphin's body temperature. Blood vessels and arteries sit just under the skin on the dorsal fins. They serve as a thermoregulator for the body, helping keep the dolphin at a constant temperature. Since dolphins are warm-blooded, or endothermic, their body temperature stays between 97 and 99°F (36–37°C). If they get too hot, the blood vessels in their dorsal fin can release heat and bring the body temperature down. It's similar to how humans sweat to lose heat. Thermoregulators are also found in the pectoral fins and the fluke, or tail. The heat from the fins is released when the dolphins swim at or near the surface of the water.

Don't Forget the Peduncle

What is the peduncle, you say? It's a muscular ridge along the back of the dolphin that stretches from the dorsal fin to the tail. It helps the dolphin maintain a straight course, but its main job is to provide extra strength to the tail. The peduncle stabilizes the tail. It also gives the tail the power for the strong strokes the dolphin needs to swim fast. Without the peduncle, dolphins probably wouldn't be able to swim so speedily. The speed produced by the strong muscles of the peduncle also helps the dolphins gain enough momentum to jump out of the water. *Whoosh!*

FIN MATCHING

HOW DO RESEARCHERS IDENTIFY DOLPHINS IN THE WILD? It's difficult. Sometimes all they see is a bit of tail or dorsal fin that might surface for just a few seconds. It is rare for dolphins or whales to completely breach (jump out of the water) when ships are around. So how do researchers know what they've seen?

It's all about the fin. Dolphins have curved or hooked dorsal fins. Porpoises have triangular dorsal fins, and whales have smaller dorsal fins. But the real identifier is how the fins look. Many dolphins have notches in their fins. This happens from playing, fighting, or maybe defending themselves from predators. Researchers keep track of the notches by taking pictures and entering them into their journals. Then, when they spot a dolphin, they compare the notches with the ones they've already seen. Sound easy? Give it a try. It's harder than it looks.

CAN YOU TELL THESE FINS APART?
MATCH THE FIN (LETTER) WITH THE ANIMAL (NUMBER).

A

B

C

1
ORCA

2
PORPOISE

3
BOTTLENOSE DOLPHIN

Answer key: 1. orca; B; 2. porpoise; C; 3. bottlenose dolphin; A.

BORROWING FROM THE DOLPHIN

WHEN YOU LOOK AT A SUBMARINE, WHAT DO YOU SEE? Is it a dolphin in disguise? Possibly.

They both have long, cylindrical bodies, a tall dorsal fin, maneuverable tail, and pectoral fins. On a submarine, the dorsal fin is called a sail. The pectoral fins are the sail planes, though they're not always located on the sides of the submarine. The rudder and propeller act together as the fluke or tail. They provide propulsion and power, just like a dolphin's tail. Did people model the submarine after some of the greatest swimmers in the ocean? Yes. It's called biomimicry, or copying an animal's features. And it works, well ... swimmingly.

A SUBMARINE'S SHAPE IS SIMILAR TO A DOLPHIN'S.

Flap That Fluke!

The biggest fin on a dolphin, porpoise, or whale is its fluke, more commonly called the tail. The tail is split into two sections and spreads out like a fan behind the animal. Tails can range in size from nine feet (2.7 m) across on an orca (which is almost the distance from the floor to a basketball hoop), to approximately 23 inches (58.4 cm) in a typical Atlantic bottlenose dolphin. Flukes can encompass almost 20 percent of the animal's total body length. So, the bigger the marine mammal, the bigger the tail!

The very muscular fluke has tips at each end that help push the water. When the tips of the tail are pointed upward, the tail is cupped and catches more water. This propels the dolphin higher and faster toward the surface. When the tips of the fluke are pointed

downward, they spread out and allow the dolphin to glide very smoothly underwater. Think of them as one giant wing, like you might see on a bird. Except this "wing" is flapped under the water instead of in the air. Similar to the dorsal fin, the flukes are made of fibrous connective tissue and do not contain any bones.

The main function of this mighty tail is propulsion: It makes the animal move. Strong tail strokes propel dolphins deep under the ocean, give them great speed, or even allow them to rise up out of the water and move forward across it.

The Skin They're In

Dolphins' skin is soft, rubbery, and smooth. Like ours, it's sensitive to the touch and fairly delicate. It's also waterproof. It has to be. Dolphins spend their entire lives in water—both salt water and freshwater. The rubbery quality of their skin makes the water roll right off. To keep

FLUKE, OR TAIL, OF A BOTTLENOSE DOLPHIN

the skin smooth and flexible, skin cells are constantly being rubbed off and replaced. That happens to humans, too. The outermost layer of a bottlenose dolphin's skin, called the epidermis, is completely replaced every two hours. That's fast! In fact, it's nine times faster than human skin cells are replaced. Since dolphins' skin cells are replaced so quickly, their skin doesn't wrinkle. There's no time for wrinkles to form.

But a dolphin's skin is not completely smooth. It has tiny bumps all over it. These bumps, called microdermal ridges, are small—so small they are practically invisible. You can only see these ridges if you get really, really close to the dolphin, or use a microscope. What is the purpose of these ridges? They trap water molecules against the dolphin's epidermis. This allows the dolphin to glide through the water more easily. That is because water molecules on the dolphin's skin are sliding against water. Two liquid surfaces move easily against each other. Without the water molecules on the dolphin's skin, the skin would be a solid object that would experience drag, or friction, when moved through water. Sound cool? It is. In fact, these microdermal ridges are so neat that some wet suit manufacturers have incorporated them into their products. This makes humans glide through the water more easily, just like a dolphin. Now, if we could only master the jumps!

CURLING RIPPLES OF TURBULENCE AS FLUIDS FLOW PAST EACH OTHER

Layers of Blubber

Dolphin skin does not just help with swimming; it also keeps the animal warm. Dolphins, whales, and porpoises have their own insulation system built right into their skin. Each animal has a layer of blubber, a kind of fat that is a part of their

GIVE IT A TRY!

TAKE A RACQUETBALL OR OTHER SMOOTH BALL and push it through the water. Do you feel the pushback? That is drag, the friction force from the water. The water molecules hit the surface of the ball and drag just slightly, causing the ball to slow down and experience resistance. Now dip or coat the ball in vegetable oil. Push it through the water again. What happens? The ball is easier to push, most likely. That is because the light coating of oil on the outside of the ball is in direct contact with the water. When two fluid objects move past each other, they simply slide and glide. This is what happens with a dolphin's skin.

ROLLS OF BLUBBER KEEP THIS BOTTLENOSE DOLPHIN WARM.

epidermis. The layer of blubber is anywhere from .75 to 1.25 inches (1.9–3.2 cm) thick. That makes it more than 10 to 20 times thicker than a similar layer in most animals living on land. Why the difference? Dolphins living in colder waters need more blubber to stay warm. The blubber helps keep the heat inside their bodies and keeps them at a toasty temperature. If they get too hot, they can always release heat from their fins.

Has Anyone Seen a Dolphin?

Why are dolphins so difficult to spot in the wild? They are constantly surfacing and diving under the water. Up, down, up, down. They also have their own built-in camouflage. That means that they blend in with the colors of their environment. The Atlantic bottlenose dolphin's skin color is gray to dark gray on its back. The gray fades to white on its lower jaw and belly. This is called countershading, and it helps hide the dolphin from both its predators and its prey. Why the two colors? When viewed from above, a dolphin's dark back blends with the dark depths. When seen from below, a dolphin's lighter belly blends with the bright sea surface.

The Eyes Have It

Dolphins have very good vision, above and below the water. Their ocular muscles, or muscles around the eyes, can bend and flex to allow the dolphin to see in both environments. Scientists believe that above the water, dolphins can see objects that are 12 to 18 feet (3.7–5.5 m) away, and underwater they can see objects around nine feet (2.7 m) away. While scientists are not sure if dolphins can see in color, it appears that their eyes may be equipped to

see a broader range of light than humans can. Dolphins, like dogs and cats, have a special layer of blue-green tissue in their eyes called tapetum lucidum. The tapetum lucidum allows the animal to see at night by gathering all available light and reflecting it back through the lens. That's helpful in the dark depths of the water.

But how do dolphins keep water out of their eyes? We humans have to wear goggles or masks to see clearly underwater. But dolphins don't. Their eyes secrete a special oil that not only gives them better vision but also keeps the water out.

Take a Look at Those Chompers

Dolphins are born with a single set of teeth. If a tooth gets knocked out or broken, there isn't a new one underneath to push itself into the gap.

Porpoises have spade-shaped teeth like humans, but dolphin and whale teeth are cone-shaped. A bottlenose dolphin can have between 72 and 104 teeth. There is an open gap in the front of their mouths where they don't have any teeth—this is so a baby dolphin won't bite its mother while nursing. Whales have between 40 and 50 teeth, while porpoises have between 60 and 120 teeth.

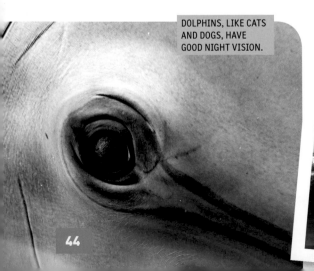

DOLPHINS, LIKE CATS AND DOGS, HAVE GOOD NIGHT VISION.

A BOTTLENOSE DOLPHIN'S SINGLE ROW OF TEETH. NOTICE THE OPEN AREA IN FRONT!

But all those teeth aren't even used for chewing! Instead, the teeth are used to grab the dolphin's prey, which it then swallows whole. Gulp!

Getting Beaky With It

Snout. Beak. Rostrum. They all mean the same thing: mouth. A rostrum can also help identify what type of cetacean you're looking at. Dolphins, for example, have a very long mouth, or rostrum. It is prominent and easy to see. Porpoises don't have a rostrum. Their beaks are smaller and rounded. Whales, like orcas, have small beaks that are more a part of their face.

A Nose Is a Nose ... Or Is It?

Dolphins don't really have noses. At least not the type of nose we humans have. Instead, dolphins have a blowhole. Just as we breathe through our nose, dolphins breathe through their blowhole. But why is it located on top of the dolphin's head? Because when dolphins, whales, or porpoises need to take a breath, they put just the top of their head above the water and inhale. If they had a nose on the front of their face, they'd have to lift their entire head out of the water to take a breath.

RING OF AGES PAST

DID YOU KNOW THAT DOLPHIN TEETH ARE BUILT IN LAYERS? Scientists have discovered that every year dolphin teeth get a new layer of enamel. Like the rings in a tree trunk, a new layer means a new ring has formed around the tooth. If you count the rings, then you'll know the age of the dolphin. It's easy to count the rings when the dolphins are young, but as they get older the rings get compressed and it's much more difficult to see them. Plus, those teeth have to be pretty hard. Imagine all of that enamel building up over the years.

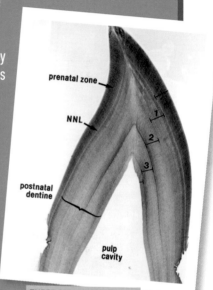

prenatal zone

NNL

postnatal dentine

pulp cavity

THREE DIFFERENT GROWTH LAYERS OF A DOLPHIN TOOTH INDICATE ITS AGE.

HAWAIIAN SPINNER DOLPHINS HAVE VERY LONG SNOUTS.

A DOLPHIN BLOWS AIR OUT OF ITS BLOWHOLE WHEN IT SURFACES.

The blowhole opens only when the cetacean needs to take a breath. When they are swimming beneath the surface, a watertight covering closes over it to keep things nice and dry. After all, no one wants to inhale water.

Chatting Up Your Friends

Dolphins also use their blowhole to communicate. They do this by pushing air through their blowhole to create a series of clicks and whistles. These sounds are in a variety of different pitches, tones, and frequencies. For example, an alarm tone might be a warning signal that a predator is approaching. Another type of click or whistle might be from a mother to its baby telling it to come closer. Meanings of clicks and whistles may be pod-specific. Their pitch and frequency may mean something to dolphins in one pod but not necessarily to another pod.

Scientists believe that each dolphin has its own signature whistle or "name." That name identifies it to the pod. The signature whistle is developed by the age of one month. A dolphin announces its "name" to other dolphins in the pod. Scientists have also observed dolphins mimicking other dolphins' signature whistles. Perhaps they use it to get the other dolphins' attention, like calling their name. Scientists aren't completely sure. Dolphin communication is very complex, and despite a lot of research, scientists aren't completely able to understand it.

Whales use clicks, whistles, pulsed calls, and even slaps of their tail on the water to communicate. The whistles and pulsed calls that sometimes sound like long, low moans are used more in social situations, perhaps to talk to other animals in the pod. Tail slaps on the water are extremely loud and might be used for warning signals or to scare fish into tighter schools for easier eating.

Porpoises appear to be less talkative than their cousins. While they do make clicking and whistling noises like dolphins, the noises are at higher pitches. Some scientists even theorize that porpoises make sounds that are too high for a human to hear. So maybe they are talking, but we just can't hear them. Like a secret code!

Navigating by Sound

The noises dolphins, whales, and porpoises make are not just to communicate. They are also important for navigation—how a dolphin determines its position and path to swim in the water. Everyone navigates. You use your eyes to see objects and move around them. When you want to head someplace new, you use a map or GPS on your smartphone. Planes use radar to check their surroundings. Radar works by sending out an electromagnetic pulse of radio waves that bounce off the objects and return to the receiver. The distance the pulse travels tells you how far away the object is located. That's a lot like echolocation.

Most of the dolphin family uses echolocation. Echolocation uses sound waves instead of radio waves. Dolphins and porpoises send out sound pulses from their melon, the fatty, rounded section of their forehead. The sound waves travel under the water until they hit an object, such as a reef. The sound pulse then bounces back to the dolphin. Scientists think

ECHOLOCATION WORKS LIKE SONAR AND HELPS A DOLPHIN LOCATE OBJECTS.

AN ORCA SLAPS THE WATER TO COMMUNICATE.

WHALES USE CLICKS, WHISTLES, PULSED CALLS, AND EVEN **SLAPS** OF **THEIR TAIL** ON THE WATER TO COMMUNICATE.

BOTTLENOSE DOLPHINS HAVE A CHAT UNDERWATER.

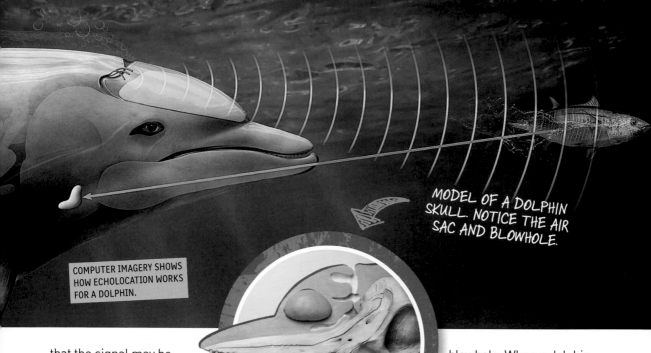

MODEL OF A DOLPHIN SKULL. NOTICE THE AIR SAC AND BLOWHOLE.

COMPUTER IMAGERY SHOWS HOW ECHOLOCATION WORKS FOR A DOLPHIN.

that the signal may be received as vibrations felt in the fatty tissue receptors of the dolphin's jaw. The signal is then transferred to the dolphin's middle and inner ears and on to the brain where it is processed. The dolphin then knows how far away the object is and immediately steers around it (or toward it, if it's a tasty fish!). Echolocation is like a dolphin's very own internal radar—no equipment required.

A Head for Echolocation

When dolphins are above the surface of the water, they can click and whistle very loudly. They can flex the muscles around the blowhole to make different sounds. But when they are underwater, the blowhole must remain closed. If it is opened underwater, water would get into their lungs and they could drown. So how do they make sound underwater?

Scientists aren't exactly sure, but they have two theories. The first idea is that dolphins have three pairs of air sacs located beneath the

blowhole. When a dolphin takes a breath, the air travels to the lungs and then back out the blowhole. But if the blowhole is closed because the dolphin is underwater, the expelled air has nowhere to go. Instead, the air goes into these open sacs. The sacs expand because they are full of air. An air plug at the end of each sac keeps the air inside. But this plug can be manipulated by the dolphin. If the dolphin allows some of the air to escape from the sac, it produces a sound. That sound travels out into the water and is used for echolocation. Hard to imagine?

Think of it this way. The air sacs are like a balloon. When empty of air, they are deflated. But when air from the lungs fills the sacs, they inflate, just like a balloon does when you blow it up. The air stays in the balloon because your fingers pinch it closed at the end. That is the air plug. As you release the air from the balloon, sometimes you hear a high whining sound. That is like the sound a dolphin makes as it releases air from the air sacs. We can't hear the sound underwater, but dolphins can.

The other theory is that there is an extra portion of fat right below the blowhole that forces the air from the air sacs in a certain direction. Just like your lips form words, this fat helps form the sounds that the dolphins release.

Which theory is correct? It is difficult to say. Scientists have not been able to see inside a dolphin's head when they are making these underwater sounds. The technology that exists to do so might harm the dolphins, and no one is willing to take that risk. For now, scientists study dolphins as much as they can and make hypotheses about what is happening.

DOLPHINS GET DIFFERENT SOUND SIGNALS FROM A CORAL REEF AND A FISH.

Fish, Reef, or Predator?

How does a dolphin know what it is "seeing" with echolocation? Every object reflects sound differently. A hard object, like a reef, would reflect a lot of the sound back. That means the vibrations would be very strong. A dolphin would know that it is "seeing" a dense, solid object. A fish is softer. That means that some of the sound waves would be absorbed by the fish. The vibrations that return to the dolphin would indicate it is a softer object. Dolphins can scan the object by repeatedly sending out sounds to determine the size, shape, speed, distance, and the direction the object is moving. They determine distance by figuring out how long it took the signal to come back to them. Scientists are not sure if dolphins form an acoustical picture, or image in their head, from the sound data they receive. They may use that data along with their vision to identify objects. Regardless of what they "see" in their head, dolphins are able to navigate with echolocation—much better than a human or even a naval ship is capable of doing.

SEEING WITH SOUND— IT'S NOT JUST FOR DOLPHINS

DOLPHINS AREN'T THE ONLY ANIMALS THAT USE ECHO-LOCATION to help them "see." Bats use it, too. Bats typically hunt for insects at night, which can make it hard to see. That is why they use echolocation—to make sure they don't run into objects or each other. Scientists have discovered that some visually impaired humans actually develop a slight ability to echolocate. By making clicking sounds, they can "see" what's in front of them and maneuver around it. Humans who have sight can be trained to do this, but only if they are blindfolded. Apparently, the human brain is more attuned to echolocation if it lacks sight.

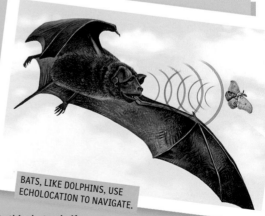

BATS, LIKE DOLPHINS, USE ECHOLOCATION TO NAVIGATE.

LEFT TO RIGHT: PORPOISE BRAIN, HUMAN BRAIN, SPERM WHALE BRAIN

DOLPHINS LEARN BY REPEATING THINGS OVER AND OVER.

TRAINERS USE WHISTLES AND GESTURES TO TELL THE DOLPHIN WHAT TO DO.

Brain Power

Which animal do you think has the biggest and most complex brain on the planet? Here's a hint. It's not a human. Both dolphins and whales have brains that are not only bigger in size but also have more folds than humans'. Have you ever seen a picture of a brain? It looks wrinkly. The wrinkles are the folds. Scientists believe that the more folds a brain has the more intelligent the animal. Does that mean that dolphins and whales are smarter than humans? No one knows for sure. An IQ test, a measure of intelligence, has not yet been accurately constructed for animals.

The one thing scientists do know is that animals with large brains, such as whales, dolphins, humans, and chimpanzees, tend to live longer. They form strong social groups and stable communities. They spend time raising their young and are capable of complex thinking and communication.

Scientists have also learned that dolphins can remember events and learn concepts. They can change their behavior based upon a reward or negative experience. For example, Kelly, a dolphin in captivity, was rewarded when she kept her enclosure clean. If a piece of paper fell into her water, she would take it to a spot in the tank to hide it. Throughout the next day, she would tear off bits of the paper and give them to the trainer one by one. Each time she did, she received a fish as a treat. Instead of turning the whole paper in at one time, and getting one fish, she had learned to spread the reward out and receive many fish. That is definitely evidence of complex thinking.

And dolphins are able to pass along what they learned to other dolphins. Kelly taught her tricks to her own calf. This shows that dolphins can communicate complicated tasks to each other. This likely happens in the wild, as well.

Further evidence of a dolphin's sophisticated brain is the animal's ability to recognize itself as an individual, much like a human does. If you saw yourself in a mirror, you'd know it was you and not someone else. Dolphins recognize themselves and each other with their own individual whistles. Dolphins are part of a very small group of animals that can do this—including some primates, some elephants, and magpies. Dolphins can mimic other animals and each other, too. If a human raises his or her arm, a dolphin will raise its pectoral fin. If one dolphin jumps high into the air, another one can repeat the same jump. These movements are all signals of the dolphin's high intelligence.

Dolphins also appear to experience basic emotions such as happiness, sadness, playfulness, and even pain. They can learn what works and what doesn't by solving problems and figuring things out. They also recognize the difference between adults and children and instinctively know that they need to be gentler with younger animals.

ORCAS HAVE BEEN KNOWN TO EAT PENGUINS.

Food for Thought

Like every living organism, for dolphins, whales, and porpoises, diet is everything. What an animal eats depends on a few factors: their nutritional needs, what is available, and the amount needed to survive. The entire toothed-whale family is carnivorous. That means that all dolphins, toothed whales, and porpoises eat meat. The types of creatures they eat depend on the species. For example, orcas eat more than 140 different kinds of animals, including many species of bony fish, sharks and rays, and about 50 different species of marine mammals. They have also been seen eating moose, penguins, leatherback sea turtles, and marine birds. When you're at the top of the food chain you can pretty much pick what you want!

Each dolphin species tends to eat the sea creatures that are naturally found in its habitat. For some species that means salmon, shrimp, krill, crab, octopus, or even jellies. Dolphins can also adapt to the food source that is available. Bottlenose dolphins living off the coast of Scotland love to eat salmon, but that fish is only available in spring and summer. So in the fall and winter, those same dolphins will eat herring or mackerel instead. A rough-toothed dolphin that lives

I'LL TAKE SOME WATER WITH THAT

DESPITE SPENDING THEIR ENTIRE LIVES IN WATER, dolphins do not actually drink water. They get all the water they need from their food. Fish, squid, and jellies naturally contain large amounts of water. When eaten, the water from the prey is absorbed into the dolphin's tissues. Since dolphins don't sweat, they don't lose water like humans do. That means they need a lot less water than many other animals, including us.

in the deep ocean will eat only squid, since that is the most abundant food source.

Porpoises have the same diet as a dolphin, which can be a problem. Dolphins have been known to attack and kill porpoises in competition for food. In addition, giant orcas are one of the most feared predators of harbor porpoises, even though both animals are members of the same family.

But I'm Still Hungry ...

The amount of food a dolphin needs to eat every day depends on what it is eating. A dolphin will eat approximately 4 to 9 percent of its weight every day. A dolphin that weighs 440 to 550 pounds (200–250 kg) needs to eat between 22 and 55 pounds (10–25 kg) of fish every day. The size, weight, and fat content of the fish determine how many a dolphin will need to eat. Fish such as mackerel and herring contain a lot of fat, so they can help fill up a dolphin fast. But squid, which have a lot less fat, will not.

Orcas will eat up to 5 percent of their body weight every day. That averages out to as much as 500 pounds (227 kg) of fish a day. With that kind of requirement, most of their time during the day is spent hunting for food. In fact, scientists have observed that, in the wild, orcas spend up to 60 percent of their day searching for food.

AN ORCA ON THE HUNT FOR ITS LUNCH

They have been known to travel hundreds of miles to search for the "perfect" meal.

You Are What You Eat

Learning what dolphins, whales, and porpoises are eating is good information for scientists to know. That way, if they capture injured animals, they know what to feed them to nurse them back to health. It's also great for those animals living or being raised in captivity. Keeping their diets as close to those of their wild counterparts is extremely important to their survival. But diet studies are now giving scientists not only an insight into what dolphins eat but also where they are doing it. By studying creatures in a particular area, scientists are using diet to determine natural habitats and environments where certain dolphin species are found.

Tracking dolphins, whales, and porpoises is not easy. They are fast, for one thing. Some species rarely surface and, when they do, they don't hang around for very long. Most whales eat while they are submerged, so it's tough to figure out exactly what they are eating. Whales also swim for miles to find food. Does that mean that area is in their natural habitat or not?

One way that scientists can learn more specifics about an animal's diet is to study what chemicals are present in its body. Humans have bits of carbon, nitrogen, oxygen, and many other compounds in the body. We need these chemicals to stay alive. They are the building blocks of our muscles, bones, organs, and brain. These chemicals come from the foods we eat.

This is true for all living organisms. Each type of animal has its own mix of chemicals within its body. These chemicals are replenished by the food that the animal eats. Hence, the term "you are what you eat." When a dolphin

DOLPHINS ARE CARNIVORES. That means they eat other animals to survive. These large, active creatures eat a lot, so they spend most of their day catching food.

Dolphins tend to work together in pods, or groups, to capture their prey. Bottlenose dolphins will herd fish into shallow, muddy waters and then smack them with their flukes. Sometimes they just flip them up into the air with their flukes and swallow the stunned fish whole. Who says you can't play with your food?

Spotted dolphins will push fish into a tight group called a bait ball that makes them easy to gobble up. Chomp!

ON THE MENU

BOTTLENOSE DOLPHIN

Found in both the Atlantic and Pacific Oceans, bottlenose dolphins love to dine on small schools of mackerel and mullet. They also love chomping on eel, shrimp, and crab.

SHRIMP

EEL

MACKEREL

SPINNER DOLPHIN

The Pacific Ocean species loves fish, jelly-fish, and krill. They can dive down to 1,000 feet (305 m) and hold their breath for up to 10 minutes to capture their prey. They really work for their food!

JELLYFISH

HERRING

HECTOR'S DOLPHIN

Some of the smallest of the dolphin species, these highly endangered animals troll the seafloor for their meals. They love to eat flounder, red cod, and crab.

FLOUNDER

CRAB

ORCA

These giant members of the dolphin family fill up their bellies with larger sea creatures. They eat sea lions, sharks, or even other whales for their dinner. If hungry enough and close to shore, they'll even grab hold of an unwary moose or deer caught swimming from one island to another.

SHARK

SEA LION

SCIENTISTS HAVE BEGUN **ANALYZING** THE **NUTRIENTS** IN DOLPHINS' TISSUES TO FIGURE OUT **WHAT** DOLPHINS ARE **EATING** AND **WHERE** THEY ARE **FINDING** IT.

A BOTTLENOSE DOLPHIN MAKES A MEAL OUT OF A REEF OCTOPUS.

A DOLPHIN SWALLOWS A SALMON WHOLE.

eats a fish, it is digested, or broken down in its stomach. A bottlenose dolphin has three stomach chambers. The first one is sort of a holding tank. The whole fish sits here until it is ready to be dissolved. When the second chamber opens, the fish slides through. Here, strong chemicals like hydrochloric acid and other enzymes digest the fish and break it up into a slushy-type mixture. (This is the same thing that happens in your stomach.) Finally, this mixture is pushed into the third chamber where the important nutrients are absorbed into the bloodstream. What's left over is waste and is pushed through the intestines and ultimately excreted from the body.

The important part of this process is absorbing nutrients. Chemicals such as carbon and nitrogen go into the blood and are transported to the dolphin's tissues and muscles. This gives the dolphin energy. It allows its muscles to flex and pump, to help the dolphin swim, jump, and dive. These nutrients in the tissue are what scientists find so fascinating. They have begun analyzing these nutrients to figure out what dolphins are eating and where they are finding it.

Follow That Isotope

Scientists have discovered that if they analyze the tissue from muscles or organs, such as from a dolphin's liver or heart, they can find certain patterns. What they are looking for are isotopes, a special type of atom. Atoms are the basic building block of all matter. Everything on Earth—including animals—is made up of hundreds of millions of atoms. Atoms contain electrons, protons, and neutrons. Most atoms have the same number of neutrons and protons. In an isotope, the atoms have a different number of neutrons.

How are isotopes used to determine where animals eat and live? Scientists take tissue samples from either living or naturally deceased animals. They find and make notes of the isotopes they find in the tissues. Then, they compare the isotopes in the dolphin with isotopes known to be in food they might have eaten. For example, if the dolphin has a carbon isotope in its muscle tissue that is known to have come from a mackerel, then the scientist can assume that the dolphin ate mackerel. Isotopes can be further identified to specific regions. A mackerel may contain an isotope that tends to be found in a specific area of the coastline or part of the ocean. The scientists can then guess that the fish came from that specific area, which would suggest the dolphin had been swimming around that area as well.

This type of research helps scientists better understand feeding habits and local habitat ranges of dolphin populations. In turn, they can use that information to help protect dolphins by knowing what areas need conservation and protection.

A RESEARCHER CHECKS A DOLPHIN'S KIDNEY AND LUNG SAMPLES TO DETERMINE HOW IT DIED.

TESTING SKIN OF A DOLPHIN TO DETERMINE ITS DNA

DEEP DIVE

MOVE LIKE A DOLPHIN

WISH YOU COULD "SEE" WHAT IT'S LIKE to be a dolphin? Give this activity a try. Grab a scarf or piece of cloth to use as a blindfold, a couple of friends, and some chairs. You will find your way throughout the room by using only your ears. Yep, that's right. You are going to "see" where you are going through echolocation.

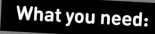

What you need:

A SCARF OR STRIP OF CLOTH

SOME CHAIRS

SOME FRIENDS

Here's how it works:

1. Pick one person to be the "dolphin." Put a blindfold on them and make them sit in the middle of the room.

2. The rest of you are "fish." You will all swim around the room in one direction.

3. Have one person stand to the side and not swim with the others. When they say "Stop," all the fish stop moving.

4. The dolphin then claps two times to send the echo. The fish respond with two claps.

5. The dolphin points to where the fish are located. The fish that are selected by the dolphin are "caught" and have to sit down.

6. The remaining fish move again. Repeat steps 4, 5, and 6 until all the fish are caught.

7. The last fish not captured becomes the next dolphin.

8. If you want to make things extra fun, give the fish various instruments to make different sounds.

A POD OF COMMON DOLPHINS STREAKS THROUGH THE WATER IN MONTEREY BAY, CALIFORNIA, U.S.A.

CHAPTER 3

A DOLPHIN'S WORLD

INTRODUCTION

DOLPHINS ARE AMAZING CREATURES.

They are some of the smartest of all marine animals and also some of the most engaging to humans. So why do we study them? Is it because they are really smart and seem to enjoy interacting with humans? Not exactly.

JUSTINE JACKSON-RICKETTS

It's because they are top predators in the ocean ecosystem. That means that they have almost no natural enemies. They prey on the smaller animals in the ocean. Other than large sharks, orcas, or humans, dolphins don't have many predators. Because they are at the top of the aquatic food chain, dolphins' health and living habits can tell us a lot about how the ocean ecosystem operates.

When I study dolphins, I look at their behavior, how they interact with one another, what they eat, and where they live. Gathering information about all of these things can help me learn more about the ocean. For instance, if dolphins have to move to a different area to find food, I want to know why. Was there something that caused the food source to disappear? Perhaps an oil spill? Too much human interaction? Or maybe the temperature changed in that area so the fish moved somewhere else? All of

these factors tell me a lot about the environment and are why studying dolphins in the wild is important. Dolphins teach us about the impacts we humans have on the ocean and the animals living within it.

Studying dolphins in captivity is a great way to learn more about their mating habits, their physical makeup, and their intelligence. By watching dolphins every day, we can learn exactly how they swim, and we can do physical exams on them to determine how their bodies work. For example, we didn't know that dolphins' pectoral fins had bones similar to those in human arms and hands until we examined a dolphin up close. We had no idea how big their brains were, or that they could learn and show emotion until scientists were able to watch them over a long period of time. Interacting with dolphins is an amazing privilege and one that many marine biologists treasure.

BOTTLENOSE
DOLPHIN

SLURPING UP SOME
FISH FOR DINNER

DOLPHINS ARE
TOP PREDATORS
IN THE OCEAN
ECOSYSTEM AND
PREY ON SMALLER
ANIMALS IN THE OCEAN.

DOLPHINS CAN BE
TAUGHT TO HOLD A BRUSH
AND PAINT PICTURES.

DOLPHINS ARE VERY
SMART AND SEEM TO
ENJOY INTERACTING
WITH HUMANS.

LEARNING AS MUCH AS WE CAN ABOUT THESE AMAZING ANIMALS IS NOT JUST FOR OUR OWN EDUCATION,

but also for learning about the entire Earth ecosystem. As some of the top predators in the ocean, dolphins can be one of the first indicators of a problem.

If we notice a problem with the dolphins in their behavior or feeding habits, that might mean there's something deeper going on. It could be because of a change in the dolphin's ecosystem. Any changes in the ocean ecosystem will ultimately affect us, since we depend on the ocean for a large part of our diet. But it's not just about food. A healthy ocean is vital for a strong global ecosystem and a prosperous planet.

Studying dolphins in the wild isn't easy. It takes time, money, and a lot of patience.

Scientists spend hours on small boats trying to find and track dolphins in all kinds of conditions. They encounter wind, rain, high seas, extreme temperatures, and storms. Sometimes they spend an entire day or two at sea without even a fin or the flip of a tail in sight. But when they do see them, those moments are worth the wait. Observing and tracking dolphins in the wild is very rewarding. It's fun, too. And researchers have discovered some amazing information.

Home Is Where the Pod Is

By observing dolphins' behavior in the wild, scientists have learned that dolphins travel in pods, or large groups. The pods are not just for social interaction but also for mating, protection, and hunting. The size of the pod depends upon the species of the animal. It also depends on the availability of food and the number of predators in their habitat. Generally, the pods that form in deep water with large open areas are larger than pods consisting of river or coastal-dwelling dolphins. Makes sense. The more room there is, the larger the party—dolphin party, that is.

The goal of every pod is to work together to raise the young, find food, and mate to keep the

RESEARCH SHIPS OFTEN ENCOUNTER ROUGH SEAS.

STUDYING DOLPHINS IN THE WILD ISN'T EASY. SCIENTISTS TRY TO FIND AND TRACK DOLPHINS IN ALL KINDS OF CONDITIONS.

THE SMALL, OLD, AND YOUNG ORCAS ARE KEPT TO THE MIDDLE OF THE POD.

species going. Dolphins don't necessarily stay with the same pod their entire life. A dolphin may live with its mother in a "nursery" pod, which is made up of mothers and their calves and occasionally older dolphins that need protecting. Sometimes up to four generations can live together in one pod. The mother dolphin returns to her family pod and continues raising her calf there. Every dolphin in the family pod helps with group "babysitting."

As the dolphin gets old enough to leave its mother, it may live in a juvenile pod for a short time. These are made up of "teenage" dolphins. Here, it's possible that two males will find their best buddies for life. These are called pair-bonds. When the juveniles have reached the right age, they may go off to find mates, and perhaps form their own pod or join a pod of adult dolphins. Male dolphins tend to move more frequently between pods. Females tend to pick a pod and stay with it for longer periods of time.

PAIR-BONDED DOLPHINS HANG OUT.

BEST BUDS

DOLPHINS ARE SOME OF THE ONLY GROUPS of animals that form lifelong bonds. Usually two male dolphins become best buds. They most likely meet in a juvenile pod or perhaps in a more mature pod, but in either case, they decide to stick together. These two friends will hunt, eat, and live together in the same pod. They work as a team to impress the females and will sometimes form a pod with just the two of them and one or two females and their calves. Scientists have noted pair-bonded males that have stuck together for 20 years or more.

A DOLPHIN CALF STICKS CLOSE TO ITS MOTHER.

WHAT'S YOUR DOLPHIN PERSONALITY?

Have you ever wondered what **TYPE OF DOLPHIN** is **MOST LIKE YOUR PERSONALITY?** Take this quiz to find out!

1. WHAT IS YOUR FAVORITE KIND OF DINNER?
a. Carnivore-style—the bigger the meat the better.
b. Fresh sushi—only the wiggliest fish will do.
c. Shrimp and maybe some crabs for extra crunch.
d. Fish eggs with a side of octopus and squid—I like my tentacles extra long.

2. HOW DO YOU FEEL ABOUT YOUR FAMILY?
a. My mom is my best friend. I like to stick close to her.
b. I prefer to hang out with a big group of my friends. The more the merrier.
c. I like my whole family to be together.
d. Just my BFFs. My besties feel like family.

3. MY FAVORITE SPOT TO LIVE IS:
a. Where it's really cold
b. I like to roam. I'm not attached to one place.
c. Warm rivers in the rain forest
d. Only warm spots in the ocean, please!

4. FASHION SENSE—WHAT COLOR SUITS ME BEST?
a. Basic black and white
b. Gray, with a pop of white
c. All over rainy-day gray!
d. Forget solids—I like stripes!

5. HOW FIT ARE YOU?
a. I am strong and powerful.
b. I'm really speedy and quite agile.
c. I'm super flexible.
d. Jumping and flipping is what I love to do.

IF YOU SCORED MOSTLY C's: You are an **IRRAWADDY DOLPHIN.** You love to dive with a small group of buddies.

IF YOU SCORED MOSTLY A's:
You are like the mighty **ORCA.** You use your great strength and cool intelligence to survive in cold places.

IF YOU SCORED MOSTLY B's:
You're a **BOTTLENOSE DOLPHIN.** You are easygoing and can live in pretty much any climate and with anyone.

IF YOU SCORED MOSTLY D's:
You're the **DUSKY DOLPHIN.** You love to hang in large groups. You flip for all those friends.

THE LEAD DOLPHIN IN A POD MAY RAKE ITS TEETH ACROSS ANOTHER DOLPHIN'S SKIN TO DEMONSTRATE DOMINANCE.

SCARS FROM RAKING

DOLPHINS WITH SCARS FROM BEING RAKED BY THE SENIOR DOLPHIN

Leader of the Pod

Just as there is a "top dog" in a pack of dogs, there is a "top dolphin" in a pod of dolphins. Typically, it is a healthy adult male dolphin. In nursery pods, however, the leader can be a female, since adult male dolphins rarely join a nursery pod. In order to become the leader, the top dolphin must demonstrate its dominance. It does this by smacking the water with its tail, snapping its jaws at the other dolphins, or even biting and chasing the other dolphins. The lead dolphin may also do what is called "raking," where it scrapes its teeth across the other dolphin's skin. This leaves behind shallow scratches or gashes on the sides of its body or head. Eventually, these scratches heal, but the scars remain. Have you ever seen small striped lines on the side of a dolphin? It's likely that it was raked by another dolphin's teeth. Leadership doesn't last very long. Sometimes it can be days or weeks. When another dolphin challenges the leader, they spar, and then the stronger one takes over.

Keeping Guard

For the most part, dolphin and whale pods are a happy, supportive society. They work together to take care of the young, protect each other, and even hunt in groups. In all of the pods except for the nursery ones, the adult male dolphins tend to swim at the edges. This may be for two reasons: to look for food and to protect the pod. They are usually the ones to fend off an attack, shielding the dolphins swimming in the middle of the pod. Those dolphins tend to be calves and older, perhaps more sickly, dolphins. Dolphins are very aware of other animals that may be injured or sick. In the wild they have been observed physically supporting another animal to keep its head above the water and breathing. In captivity, dolphins will make clicking noises or whistles to get a trainer's attention for a sick or injured friend.

The males at the edge of the pod may also act as scouts, swimming ahead to survey the water. Are they scouting for food or for predators? Scientists aren't sure. But these scouts report back to the leader what they have learned.

Group Feeding

Dolphins work together to find and capture food. Scientists call this herding. When they find a school, or group, of fish to eat, the pod will swim around and around it, forcing the fish into a tight group. The close-packed school of fish makes an easy grab-and-go meal. The dolphins simply swim through one at a time, grab a fish in their mouth, and go out the other side of the school. Chomp! This is known as circular cooperative feeding.

BOTTLENOSE DOLPHINS USE A MUD RING TO HERD AND CAPTURE FISH.

Other dolphins will get together as a group and stun the fish with their tails. Whap! They beat their flukes against the water, knocking out the fish in the process. Then they scoop them up for a quick meal. Sometimes dolphins in the wild work in tandem with fishermen. They herd fish toward the nets. The fish that escape become an afternoon or mid-morning snack for the lucky dolphin. Dolphins will occasionally break up into small groups of about three or four and swim at the fish from different angles. One small group may herd the fish toward the other group of dolphins. The fish get confused and suddenly are surrounded on all sides. An easy meal for the dolphins! This is known as zigzag cooperative feeding.

In areas near the coastline, dolphins have been known to herd fish toward the shore's shallow waters. Scientists call this front cooperative feeding. When the fish become stranded, the dolphins swoop in and eat them. The danger

DOLPHIN BIZ

THE COOPERATION IN A DOLPHIN POD is so unique and works so well that many businesses are trying to adopt the same idea. Only this time, with humans! The leaders figure that if they can teach people in their office to work together on a project, feel the happiness of a community, and use their group thinking as a positive force, the company will thrive. Not a bad idea. Just as long as there is no raking of teeth involved.

DOLPHINS THAT SWIM TOGETHER, WORK WELL TOGETHER.

IN AREAS NEAR THE COASTLINE, DOLPHINS HAVE BEEN KNOWN TO HERD FISH TOWARD THE SHORE'S SHALLOW WATERS.

A POD OF HUMPBACK WHALES USES BUBBLES TO TRAP THEIR FOOD.

SHARK ATTACK!

DOLPHINS DO NOT NORMALLY ATTACK SHARKS unless they are attacked first. Sharks, for the most part, are too smart to take on an entire dolphin pod. If they do approach a dolphin, it is usually a young or sick one. Scientists have seen three dolphins head-butt sharks in their tender stomach region to fend off an attack on a weaker dolphin. Despite what you may have heard, though, dolphins don't protect humans from sharks.

SHARKS, WHILE TOP PREDATORS, USUALLY LEAVE DOLPHINS ALONE.

is that the dolphins can strand themselves. They have to be careful not to go into water that is too shallow so that they can swim back out to sea when they are done eating.

Since they are so intelligent, dolphins will sometimes change which feeding method they use. They have even been observed using more than one method at the same time. They might start with the circular method and then add in the zigzag to confuse the fish. Scientists have also noticed that some pods tend to use the same methods over and over. They think that may be because the older dolphins have taught the younger ones their favorite method. Regardless of which method they use, or how they do it, the goal is the same: Get the food!

Bubbles and Balls

Dolphins aren't the only aquatic mammals that work together to find food. Whales do it, too. A group of humpback whales has been known to use bubbles from their blowholes to herd fish into a tight circle. The whales swim deep below the fish and shoot

bubbles up at them. The bubbles act like a net, surrounding the fish and pushing them together. When the fish are in a nice, compact circle, the whales open their mouths wide and scoop them into their gaping jaws.

Orcas have been seen creating what scientists call a bait ball. They swim round and round the fish, pushing them into a circle, and then whap them with their giant tails! The stunned fish aren't even aware that they've just become an orca snack.

A BOTTLENOSE DOLPHIN USES A SPONGE TO HELP CAPTURE ITS FOOD.

Using Tools to Capture Food

Dolphins have come up with other ingenious ways to capture prey. They sometimes use tools to help them find food. This tends to happen more when the dolphin is looking for food on its own. The Australian bottlenose dolphin is particularly good at this. Scientists have observed a single Australian bottlenose dolphin using a conch shell, a large rounded shell, to scoop up fish.

NEED A LIFT?

A COUPLE OF SCIENTISTS got the thrill of a life-time when they saw a humpback whale slowly lifting a bottlenose dolphin out of the water. They even captured a video of it! Why the lift? The researchers aren't sure. Although they were a fair distance away, it didn't look like the dolphin was injured. The humpback also didn't appear to be aggressive or trying to hurt the dolphin. Maybe they were just having fun and seeing how high they could go. Regardless, it looked like they were having a whale of a time!

A DOLPHIN AND A WHALE APPEAR TO PLAY.

The dolphin carried the conch shell in its teeth and dove deep under the water. When it surfaced, it shook the shell back and forth to remove the water, and the fish trapped inside the shell flew into its mouth. Gulp!

In another case, Australian bottlenose dolphins have been seen using sea sponges to poke fish out of their hiding holes. The fish most likely sense the dolphins and go into small bits of coral or hide under the sandy seabed. The dolphin then holds a sea sponge in its beak and uses it to poke around. The fish is pushed out or comes out to see what's going on. The dolphin quickly drops the sponge and gobbles up the fish. Then it grabs the sponge and searches for yet another fish to poke.

Being Social

Occasionally a dolphin—or a whole pod—swims by a research vessel to say hello. And there have been incidents of a dolphin pod swimming near surfers off the shores of England and Australia. How cool is that? But it doesn't happen too often, and only certain species of dolphins are that friendly to—or curious about—humans.

What should you do if approached by a dolphin? Stay calm, but get out of its way. Dolphins in the wild are not trained animals; you don't know what they will do. They are very strong, and even though they seem friendly, they can harm you. Do not pet or feed a dolphin. In fact, it is illegal to feed them in the wild. Try to stay at least 50 feet (15 m) away from any dolphin at all times. If they show interest in your bait or fishing lines, pull in your fishing gear and move away. You don't want to entangle the dolphin—if it gets caught, it could get pulled underwater for too long and won't be able to breathe.

Humans aren't the only animals with whom dolphins spend their time. Pods of dolphins have been seen swimming with other dolphin species, gray whales, humpbacks, and even right whales. Why do these species swim together? Researchers don't know. Perhaps they just find it fun to pal around with bigger animals. They've never been seen hunting or feeding together.

THE SUN SETS OVER A POD OF BOTTLENOSE DOLPHINS.

A GROUP OF DOLPHINS CATCH A WAVE TOGETHER. SURF'S UP!

SIX IMPORTANT LIFE LESSONS WE CAN LEARN FROM DOLPHINS

DOLPHINS HAVE EXHIBITED all of these traits in their pods. They are cooperative communities that work together to promote harmony within the pod and their environment. No wonder businesses want to mimic them. Dolphins make great role models!

1. Compassion
2. Patience
3. Responsibility
4. Respect for Elders
5. Working Together
6. Taking Care of Each Other

To the Rescue

Sometimes a whale or dolphin strands itself and gets stuck on land. Animal rescue organizations then spring into action and help the animal get back into the ocean. Scientists believe that strandings can be accidental, perhaps caused when the animal swims too close to shore for food. It is also possible that sick and dying animals purposely strand themselves onshore. Occasionally, there are mass strandings of a whole pod of whales or dolphins. Is it because an injured animal went ashore first and the others didn't want to leave it? Or did noise pollution in the ocean drive them to a beach? No one knows for sure, but it is certainly a sad sight.

Animal rescue workers keep the animal calm, wet, and tipped up so that it can breathe. They sometimes spend hours digging in the sand to shift the creature back into the water. If the animal is injured, they may decide to take it to their center to treat it. The injured animals are rehabilitated and released back into the ocean as soon as possible. Occasionally, the injury is too severe for the animal to survive in the wild. These animals might then become permanent members of local marine museums or aquatic centers.

A 10-DAY-OLD BABY DOLPHIN THAT WAS CAUGHT IN A FISHING NET GETS A BATH AT A MARINE ANIMAL RESCUE CENTER.

Capturing Dolphins in the Wild

Until the late 20th century, the capture of dolphins from the wild was not controlled by the government. People would herd several dolphins from the same pod, using helicopters that moved the animals toward boats, where they were captured by nets. The dolphins were then kept wet and calm while they were sent to their new homes, such as marine amusement centers. The same process was used to capture whales and orcas. Once they reached their new homes, the

VOLUNTEERS ASSIST PILOT WHALES DURING A MASS STRANDING.

animals were introduced into enclosures and then to their human trainers, who taught them to put on shows for millions of cheering fans.

Dolphins and whales are now protected by government regulations in many places. These regulations say that you cannot capture a dolphin without a special permit from the government. Only approved facilities may obtain a permit. Harassing, harming, killing, or feeding wild dolphins is prohibited under the U.S. Marine Mammal Protection Act of 1972. These regulations make it much more difficult to obtain a healthy, wild dolphin and keep it captive. That is why breeding programs at marine amusement centers have grown. Still, more than 5,000 dolphins, whales, and porpoises have been captured over the last 30 years. Most of them have been used in aquariums for research or entertainment, and some have been used by the military. Almost three-quarters of these captive dolphins are female. For the most part, these animals appear to adapt to captivity well, although their life span can be shorter than it would be in the wild.

WHAT TO DO IF YOU ENCOUNTER A STRANDED ANIMAL

1. **CALL FOR HELP.** In the United States, you can call the Whale Dolphin Conservation national hotline. Notify local lifeguard stations or police.
2. **BE VERY CAREFUL** if you approach it. These are wild creatures and possibly in pain. They may hurt you without meaning to or in self-defense.
3. **IF YOU ARE COMFORTABLE** with approaching the animal, the first thing to do is to make sure the blowhole is open and unobstructed so that the animal can breathe.
4. **IF YOU CAN POUR WATER SAFELY** over the animal, do so, being careful not to get the water into the blowhole.
5. **DO NOT ATTEMPT TO DRAG** the animal back into the water. This could hurt it and you.
6. **KEEP PEOPLE AND DOGS AWAY** so as not to stress the animal. Do find a few adults to help.
7. **WAIT FOR EXPERT HELP** at a safe distance. Remember these are powerful, wild creatures.

A STRANDED PILOT WHALE MOTHER AND CALF LIE IN SHALLOW WATER.

TWO RESEARCHERS COME TO THE AID OF A STRANDED DOLPHIN.

TRY TO STAY AT LEAST 50 FEET (15 M) AWAY FROM ANY DOLPHIN AT ALL TIMES.

TOURISTS GET AN UP-CLOSE LOOK AT A POD OF DOLPHINS OFF THE COAST OF BAJA, CALIFORNIA, U.S.A.

DOLPHIN SPOTTING

WANT TO SEE DOLPHINS IN THEIR NATURAL HABITAT? It's great fun, but make sure that you pick an eco-friendly dolphin or whale-watching boat tour that does the following:

- Keeps a respectful distance from habitats and does not approach or feed the animals. Dolphins and whales can be injured by a boat that comes too close.
- Limits the time spent in the habitat so as not to interfere with the animals' natural feeding process.
- Uses clean energy in the area and doesn't dump trash.
- Includes a trained educator who explains what guests are seeing.
- For more information, check out Whale SENSE or Dolphin SMART programs, which list the tours that are the best ones for both humans and marine mammals.

Training Dolphins

Dolphins learn fast and love to be stimulated by different tasks. When a dolphin is first brought into captivity, the trainers will slowly introduce themselves to the dolphin. Next, the dolphins are given easy tasks and rewarded with fish. The goal is to teach the dolphins using positive reinforcement: When they perform a task properly, they are rewarded. This method works quite well with intelligent mammals. Dolphins are quick to pick up on new tricks and have even been known to come up with their own just to get a treat.

When trainers teach dolphins tricks such as jumping, twisting, and bowing, they are reinforcing habits that the dolphins would do in the wild. "Walking" across the water on their fluke, slapping their fluke, and waving their pectoral fins are all actions that have been observed in the wild. When trainers have two dolphins swim next to each other and jump together, that happens in the wild, too. The idea is to keep the dolphins active by doing tricks but to also allow them to behave as they would in their natural habitat.

Target and Recall

Trainers use two tools to help the dolphins learn new behaviors. The first one is the target. A target is something that the dolphin will focus on during training. It can be the trainer's palm, a ball, or even an object at the end of a stick. The target is held near the dolphin, and whenever they touch it with their rostrum, they receive a reward. Once the dolphin understands that action, the target is moved to a new position. The behavior is repeated until the dolphin learns to move to a new target position. Trainers slowly build upon this behavior until they have the dolphins doing complex moves. Ever been to a marine park and watched a dolphin show? Most likely you have seen the trainer stick their palm out for the dolphin to nudge. Watch it happen next time and note when the dolphin does it. Most likely it is before and after a trick.

Trainers also use whistles to enhance the training. The sound combined with the target reinforces the behavior. Whistles are also used for recall. Recall is a specific behavior that makes the dolphin stop what it is doing and return to a specific point. Usually, that is the

TRAINED DOLPHINS MOVE IN TANDEM TO COMMANDS.

A BOTTLENOSE DOLPHIN GETS INSTRUCTIONS FROM ITS TRAINER.

YOU CAN BECOME A DOLPHIN TRAINER

EVER DREAMED OF WORKING WITH DOLPHINS? Maybe you want to train them to do tricks. Here are the steps you'll need to take to become a dolphin trainer:

1 GAIN EXPERIENCE WITH ANIMAL HANDLING FROM EXPERTS. Volunteer at your local zoo, veterinary offices, animal shelters, or marine aquatic centers.

2 CONSIDER LEARNING TO TRAIN ANIMALS when you are in high school. Help to raise a guide dog. Work with rehabilitation centers to train their animals for release back into the wild.

3 GO TO COLLEGE and get your bachelor's degree. Study any life science topic, such as biology, zoology, marine biology, or animal science.

4 EARN A SCUBA CERTIFICATION. If you're going to be in the water with dolphins, you need to know how to scuba dive.

5 EARN A CPR AND FIRST AID CERTIFICATION. This is to take care of yourself or other trainers if necessary.

6 GET EXPERIENCE! Be enthusiastic and open to constructive criticism, and just have fun!

trainer. When the dolphin hears the recall signal, like a whistle or a hand slap on the water, it immediately proceeds to the agreed-upon point. Teaching dolphins to target and recall is not easy. It can take months to achieve. But it is a very effective way to keep the dolphin stimulated and promotes a strong relationship between dolphin and trainer. More importantly, it can keep the dolphins safe. If the trainer needs the dolphin to move away from a danger or toward a safe point, the recall signal ensures the dolphin responds immediately.

Keeping Them Healthy

Trainers take every precaution to keep their dolphins and whales healthy. Every animal has routine medical checkups. Trainers work daily with the animals so that they learn to be comfortable and calm during all procedures. Dolphins and whales are trained to present a part of their body when asked for it. For example, if the vet needs to see the underside of the dolphin, the trainer will give the signal for the dolphin to flip over. The dolphin learns to do that on command and is rewarded with a fish. Animals are trained to hold still while being examined. This allows doctors to take ultrasounds or x-rays without having to put the animal to sleep with anesthesia or drugs. Detailed records of the animal's health, both physical and mental, are kept at all times. Any time a trainer notices something that might be wrong or a little bit out of the ordinary, he or she informs the medical team. The goal is to keep the animals as healthy and happy as possible.

Keeping the animals healthy also means feeding them the appropriate diet. Dolphins are fed fish and squid that have been caught fresh and frozen. The

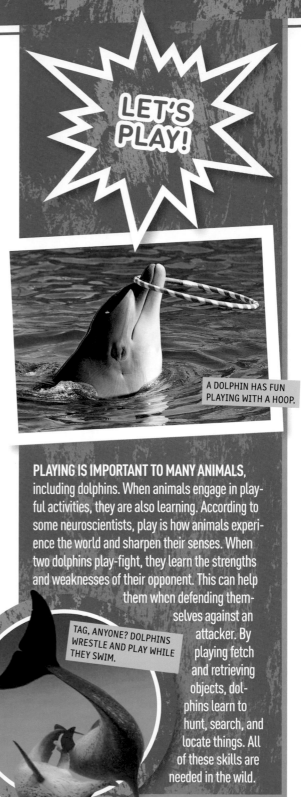

LET'S PLAY!

A DOLPHIN HAS FUN PLAYING WITH A HOOP.

PLAYING IS IMPORTANT TO MANY ANIMALS, including dolphins. When animals engage in playful activities, they are also learning. According to some neuroscientists, play is how animals experience the world and sharpen their senses. When two dolphins play-fight, they learn the strengths and weaknesses of their opponent. This can help them when defending themselves against an attacker. By playing fetch and retrieving objects, dolphins learn to hunt, search, and locate things. All of these skills are needed in the wild.

TAG, ANYONE? DOLPHINS WRESTLE AND PLAY WHILE THEY SWIM.

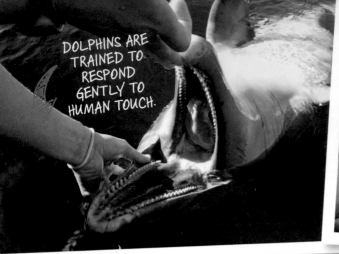

DOLPHINS ARE TRAINED TO RESPOND GENTLY TO HUMAN TOUCH.

DOLPHINS ARE INSPECTED DAILY TO ENSURE THEY ARE HEALTHY.

food is allowed to thaw so it's not frozen when the dolphins eat it. The amount of food fed to each dolphin or whale depends upon the species. Each dolphin has its own carefully labeled food canister. Strict records are kept of how much food each animal eats every day.

The enclosures are kept clean. They have complex water filtration systems to remove waste and refresh the water. Dolphins urinate about one gallon (3.8 L) per day. That's about three times as much as the average human between the ages of 8 and 14. In a tank that holds tens of thousands of gallons of water, that may not seem like much, but the water still needs to be cleaned. Dolphins also produce about three pounds (1.4 kg) of feces every day. The feces looks like a cloud of thin green liquid, which doesn't dissolve well in water. Typically, the water filtration system will remove all of this from the tank. If it doesn't, chemicals determined to be safe for the dolphins are added to the enclosure to help purify the water. Pools also generally have a vacuum system to remove debris, and the glass walls are scrubbed down with a brush periodically to prevent algae buildup.

A VETERINARIAN DRAWS BLOOD FROM A DOLPHIN'S FLUKE.

Breeding Dolphins

A large majority of the dolphins in captivity come from breeding programs. These are similar to the breeding programs found in many zoos. Calves that are produced through these programs are kept together with their mother, just like they would be in the wild. The calves are introduced to trainers fairly early on and learn that the trainers are a part of their family. Many organizations are not thrilled with captive dolphin breeding programs. That is because the family structure in captivity is forced upon the dolphins. In the wild, they are allowed to roam and choose their own pods. Yet most aquariums and marine centers take very good care of the new dolphin calves and their mothers. Breeding programs continue to thrive.

The Debate Over Captivity

There is much debate about whether dolphins, porpoises, and whales belong in captivity. While trainers and researchers do their best to take good care of the animals, the tanks where they live clearly restrict their overall movement. In the wild, a whale or dolphin might swim up to 100 miles (161 km) a day. Naturally, their tanks are not that big. Even newly proposed larger tanks for orcas at some entertainment centers won't be big enough. That's because an orca can dive up to 1,000 feet (305 m).

The opponents of aquatic centers say that the animals are subjected to problems they wouldn't encounter in the wild. They are separated from their families. They are trained to do tricks in entertainment shows, and they forget many of their natural instincts for hunting and communicating. Some even believe that since dolphins are so intelligent, keeping them captive is cruel and affects their emotional outlook on life.

TRAINING DOLPHINS WITH COMPLEX PUZZLES STIMULATES THEIR THINKING.

Learning From Captive Dolphins

And yet, there are positive reasons why dolphins, porpoises, and whales remain in captivity. Observing dolphins under controlled situations such as a tank enclosure has given researchers a lot of information about these amazing mammal species. For example, they have seen up close how dolphins swim, dive, and play. They have recorded thousands of hours of communication sounds in the forms of clicks, whistles, and fluke slaps. By piecing this information together, scientists can distinguish particular speech patterns among the animals.

Through observation and testing, researchers

YOU CAN BE A MARINE MAMMAL VETERINARIAN

LOVE TO WORK WITH ANIMALS AND TAKE CARE OF THEM? Think dogs and cats are boring? Why not become a marine mammal veterinarian! You will be able to take care of all of the animals at aquarium and marine mammal centers, such as penguins, walruses, sea lions, orcas, dolphins, and porpoises. It's a great job. Of course, you'll have to go to college and get a degree. Then four years of veterinary school. That's where you'll learn about many different animals and how their bodies work, inside and out. You may then go into practice at an aquarium. You might do more training under an established marine veterinarian, just to get you used to the animals. You will learn how to give them physical exams and vaccinations, take x-rays, and even perform surgeries if needed. The whole time you will be helping some amazing aquatic animals to stay healthy. If this sounds like something you'd like to do, look for more information about colleges and universities that offer marine mammal studies. Then research veterinary schools. Dive into a great career!

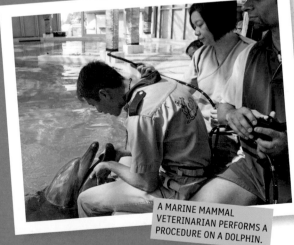

A MARINE MAMMAL VETERINARIAN PERFORMS A PROCEDURE ON A DOLPHIN.

ORGANIZATIONS THAT PROTECT

MANY ORGANIZATIONS EXIST TO ENSURE THE PROTECTION and safe care of dolphins and other marine animals. The Association of Zoos and Aquariums (AZA) is one of the largest. Their mission is to teach humans to value and respect marine life, and to help wildlife and all wild environments. Member zoos and aquariums promise to maintain high health standards, clean tanks, and excellent training for their animals. Most of these places offer education classes for kids and adults to learn more about dolphins and whales. They teach about conservation practices such as beach cleanups, the type of fish to eat in support of the ocean, and also how the animals should be treated in the wild. AZA is just one of the many organizations that work to protect, conserve, and inform.

DOLPHINS ARE RESCUED AND RELEASED AFTER A TWO-MONTH RECOVERY IN KEY LARGO, FLORIDA, U.S.A.

THE AQUARIUM OF THE PACIFIC, IN LONG BEACH, CALIFORNIA, U.S.A., IS HOME TO MORE THAN 11,000 PACIFIC OCEAN ANIMALS.

have begun to understand how a dolphin uses echolocation to navigate the world around them. They have witnessed the broad range of dolphin emotions: anger, sadness, or compassion for other animals. They have learned how to successfully keep dolphins healthy for long periods of time and also how to breed them.

All of this information is used not only to further our understanding of these creatures but also to help save them. What scientists have learned from captive dolphins has helped increase conservation efforts in the wild. Specifically, the survival rate of mass strandings is up from 10 percent to 30 percent over the last decade. Increased knowledge about dolphins also helps educate people and inspire respect. People are taught that approaching a dolphin in the wild is not a good idea, but watching them from a safe distance is fine.

That allows dolphins to live without interference, as they should.

Back to the Wild

It is rare for captive dolphins to be released back into the wild, but there are successful reintroduction stories. In one instance, a group of researchers took two male dolphins that had been in captivity at a resort in Turkey to a new training facility. They spent more than a year teaching them how to live in the wild. The dolphins, called Misha and Tom, had to learn how to hunt on their own. They had been trained to only eat fish that were placed into their mouths by humans, so when the researchers filled their new tanks with fish, Tom and Misha did nothing. They didn't even appear to notice that the fish were there. The trainers slowly taught Tom and Misha how to capture the fish on their own. As soon as the dolphins mastered this, the next step was to remove human contact. Over a period of time, the humans disappeared from the dolphins' sight. Tom and Misha had to fend for themselves.

Finally, the big day arrived. Tom and Misha were released into the Aegean Sea, near the spot where they were originally believed to have been caught. They took off through the waves. The researchers equipped them with tracking devices to watch their progress. Within 48 hours of their release, Tom and Misha had traveled more than 100 miles (161 km). They were spotted successfully hunting and even interacting with other wild dolphins. Researchers thought that they might be looking for their original pod. More than two years later, the dolphins appear to still be doing well.

DEEP DIVE

DOLPHIN DETECTION

EVERYONE LOVES DOLPHINS? It's true. People have a fascination with these aquatic creatures. Take a look around the next time you're outside. You may just spot a dolphin in your travels. Can you see any in these pictures?

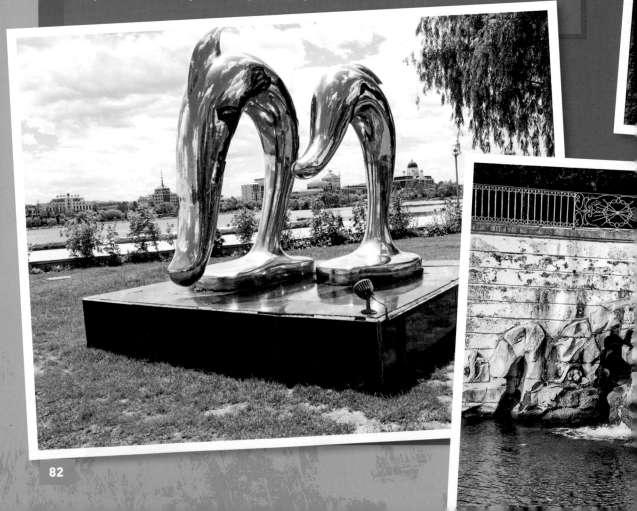

82

TWO DOLPHINS RACE A
WHALE-WATCHING BOAT.

CHAPTER 4

DOLPHINS AND HUMANS TOGETHER

INTRODUCTION

HUMANS AND DOLPHINS MUST LEARN TO COEXIST ON THIS PLANET.

I believe that is possible, and I am passionate about it. Through my research, I have been able to determine the general habitats of Irrawaddy dolphins in the Gulf of Thailand.

JUSTINE JACKSON-RICKETTS

A great way to learn more about dolphins' habitat is to study their diet. I analyze stranded dolphins, ones that have washed up on shore or are found floating in the water. I take samples of their skin and teeth and perform experiments to figure out what types of chemicals are present. The types of chemicals tell me what kind of food the dolphins have eaten. By noting where and when the dolphins have been found and then searching for their food sources, I can make a "habitat map" of where Irrawaddy dolphins live and what they eat.

In the diet study, we determined what type of prey makes up the majority of their food. When we compare that to the information we gathered in tracking the dolphins, we can pinpoint the areas where they most likely feed. Those areas will be the places where humans, particularly fishing boats and ecotourism boats, should avoid. We work closely with the Thai government to accomplish the same goal:

to set up protected areas for the dolphins where no boats can enter. This will give Irrawaddy dolphins a safe place to hunt, eat, and reproduce.

With fewer fishermen around, other marine mammals, fish, and plants would also benefit, contributing to a rich, healthy ecosystem. The incidents of bycatch—the accidental capture of marine mammals in fishing lines or nets—would be greatly reduced. The competition for fish between human and dolphin would all but disappear in this protected area. Is this possible? We hope so. It is up to each government to regulate the laws surrounding their native waters. In some areas of the world, marine-protected areas are already in place. They are showing evidence that humans and dolphins can peacefully coexist and have a more beneficial environment. It is my hope that continued research and education will help these amazing aquatic creatures prosper on our planet.

AN IRRAWADDY DOLPHIN STOPS BY FOR A QUICK SNACK.

IN SOME AREAS OF THE WORLD, MARINE-PROTECTED AREAS EXIST WHERE NO BOATS CAN ENTER.

SMALL BOAT TOURS ON THE MEKONG RIVER TAKE TOURISTS TO SEE IRRAWADDY DOLPHINS.

SINCE ANCIENT TIMES, HUMANS HAVE BEEN CAPTIVATED BY DOLPHINS.

Ancient Greeks called them *hieros ichthys*, or "sacred fish." They believed that good luck came to those who encountered a pod of dolphins at sea. It was against the law to hurt or kill a dolphin, a crime punishable by death.

Today, humans still find dolphins inspiring and fascinating and want to protect them. And who wouldn't? Their sleek, slim bodies that jump high into the air; their enigmatic smiles that seem to express a joy for life; their true community living that enhances everyone in their pod ... Dolphins are truly amazing mammals. To ensure that these animals can continue to be one of Earth's most treasured creatures, millions of dollars are spent every year on research, upkeep, and conservation efforts.

Fossil Finds

Whale, dolphin, and porpoise research facilities are found all over the world. Scientists study these animals both in the field and in captivity, at marine mammal centers and aquariums. But research is also done with fossils.

When you hear the term "paleontologist," you probably think of scientists who study dinosaurs. But dinosaurs aren't the only prehistoric fascination for paleontologists. Some study ancient cetaceans. Shark-toothed dolphins, ancient river dolphins, and even whales that "walk" have all been uncovered by paleontologists in places around the world.

In a small desert near the coast of southern Peru, three species of ancient dolphins were uncovered. Wait. Dolphins in a desert? Not exactly. While it's a desert now, scientists believe

SAVE THAT ROCK!

A TINY, WEIRDLY SHAPED PEBBLE WASHED ashore on a beach near Camp Lejeune, North Carolina, U.S.A. It didn't look like much, just a bit of twisted rock. Thankfully, it was not thrown away. Instead, the rock was sent to the Smithsonian Institution. Years later, the rock was picked up and studied by paleontologist Dr. Travis Park. Turns out this twisted bit of rock was really a tiny ear bone from a xenorophid, an ancient type of dolphin that lived more than 26 million years ago. The ear bone is very similar to those seen in present-day dolphins. Dr. Park and his team are studying the bone and think that it may eventually hold the key to understanding how echolocation works in cetaceans. What a lucky find!

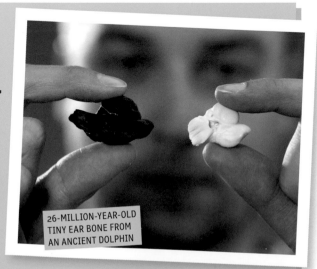

26-MILLION-YEAR-OLD TINY EAR BONE FROM AN ANCIENT DOLPHIN

that more than 16 million years ago this area was part of the South Pacific Ocean. These three skeletons, two with completely preserved skulls, are the first of their kind to be found fairly intact. Dubbed squalodelphinids, the dolphins appear to be related to the endangered South Asian river dolphin. This rare find is just one example of the many discoveries that hold the key to how cetaceans have evolved.

GPS TRACKING CAMERA ATTACHED TO A DOLPHIN

Humans and Dolphins Today

Studying dolphin fossils is just one of the hundreds of research projects underway. Researchers like Justine spend days huddled on tiny boats following dolphins around the world. Many of these studies consist of observing and taking notes. Some include capturing the dolphins and placing GPS trackers on them. Other projects require dolphins to be caught humanely, and blood and tissue samples are taken for testing. Regardless of which type of project is being conducted, the primary thought is the dolphins' health and welfare.

In Justine's study, the research boats stay a safe distance from the dolphins and are careful not to interfere with their normal activities. They don't want to scare the dolphins or cause them to swim into fishing nets or shallow areas where they can't get out. The researchers use equipment to observe the dolphins and take many notes and pictures to review later. Justine's research takes place in the waters near Thailand, and the Thai government prohibits the scientists from interfering with live dolphins. That means they are not able to get active tissue and blood samples. It is

PREHISTORIC DOLPHIN FOSSIL

A DAY IN THE FIELD WITH JUSTINE JACKSON-RICKETTS

GETTING READY

- Wake up early
- Breakfast with the team
- Make sure everything's charged, packed up, ready to go
- Pile in the truck and head to the pier (one of three)
- Load everything on the boat and assign positions
- Get out to the starting point
- On the way, get data sheets ready and make sure GPS devices are powered up

OUR RESEARCH BOAT IS LOADED AND READY TO HEAD OUT TO THE WATER.

GATHERING DATA

- Start transect line—the path that we will follow—with environmental readings
- Follow the line, counting boats and fixed-gear markers and taking GPS points for each count
- Stop when observer sees dolphins and take environmental readings. Determine number, group composition, and behavior of dolphins. Make decision to follow dolphins or continue on line. If able to gather info without following, carry on. If not, follow until data collected.

AN IRRAWADDY DOLPHIN SPLASHES ABOVE THE WATER.

- If no dolphins, stop and take environmental readings every 30 minutes
- Finish line, take environmental readings
- Start next line and repeat procedures
- Break for lunch about noon
- Back on effort until water gets too choppy or it starts to get dark

HEADING HOME

- Pack up while heading back in; make sure sheets are organized and packed away safely
- Get back in and move gear from boat to truck
- Head back to resort
- Shower
- Have dinner with team
- Download data from GPS devices and environmental readers
- Start all batteries charging
- Input data from datasheets into computer and upload all data to the cloud
- Sleep and repeat

OUR RESEARCH BOAT AT SUNSET

IT IS **IMPORTANT** FOR RESEARCHERS TO HAVE A **COOPERATIVE RELATIONSHIP** WITH **LOCAL GOVERNMENTS** SO THAT **RESEARCH** IS **SUPPORTED.**

important for researchers to follow the directions of local governments. They need to have a cooperative relationship so that their research is supported and respected.

Part of the research involves learning about the dolphins' diet. Since they are not allowed to touch live dolphins, scientists must rely on recovering dolphins that may have been killed naturally or in fishing nets. If they happen to encounter a deceased dolphin, they will take it back to their lab to perform tests on it. The results are used to learn about the habitats where the dolphins live and find food. The goal of this research is to gain information about the Irrawaddy dolphins and pass it along to the Thai governments so that they can support the dolphin's natural environment.

Listening In

Several researchers have created tools to try to crack the code on dolphin communication. One such electronic device records and then plays back dolphin calls, whistles, and clicks. The idea is to make a sound with the device and see how the dolphin responds. That will help the researchers figure out what that sound means. The research can take many years since each dolphin has its own unique sounds and communication.

Still, the scientists are hopeful that this may help humans "talk" to a dolphin one day.

Another project that hopes to achieve the same goal involves the use of a handheld electronic tablet. Dolphin researcher Jack Kassewitz devised an app that one dolphin, named Merlin, is actually using to communicate. Merlin has been taught to look at images and touch his rostrum to the screen when he recognizes something. Examples of the images include a yellow duck, a ball, or a circle. The key is that when Merlin touches the screen, he usually makes a noise—a click or whistle. The tablet records this noise and associates it with the symbol. Over the course of many months, Jack was able to form a big vocabulary bank of words and sounds. These can hopefully one day be translated into a type of interactive language with dolphins.

Dolphins are very intelligent and catch on quickly to these games. Imagine a dolphin working with an electronic tablet. That would be strange to see, wouldn't it? Maybe not. Dolphins have shown that they can understand up to sixty or more words. Put together, those words could make about 2,000 different sentences. That's a fairly complex understanding of our language. Now if we could only understand what they are saying back to us!

A RESEARCHER LISTENS IN ON DOLPHIN CHATTER WITH RECORDING EQUIPMENT.

TRAINER JACK KASSEWITZ TEACHES MERLIN THE DOLPHIN HOW TO USE A TABLET.

CHAT-TING WITH DOLPHINS

DOLPHIN RESEARCHER DENISE HERZING has spent more than 30 years of her life in the water with dolphins. Her mission is to understand their language and communicate with them. Her years of research have paid off. Herzing and her fellow researchers have created an electric keyboard that acts as a two-way communication device between dolphins and humans. It is called CHAT (Cetacean Hearing and Telemetry). This waterproof computer device can detect the sound a dolphin makes and transmit it to a diver who is underwater. This is so the diver can hear what the dolphin is saying. Eventually, the diver transmits a sound back to the dolphin from the hundreds of noises stored on CHAT. Denise is trying to convey her own unique whistle to the dolphins and get them to recognize that whistle as her. She is also working on teaching the dolphins to recognize objects and words. Dolphins are natural mimics, so they will sometimes repeat back the sound. The thing is, she's not sure if they understand what they are saying or if they are just mimicking. Still, this technology seems very promising and may one day break the communication barrier between humans and dolphins.

RESEARCHER DENISE HERZING ATTEMPTS TO COMMUNICATE WITH DOLPHINS USING WHISTLES.

Military Helpers

Research can help us learn more about cetaceans, but it can also go one step further: It can help humans to mimic these species' unique abilities. The U.S. Navy has been researching marine mammals since the 1960s. Their goal is to learn all they can about how dolphins and beluga whales use sonar. They have used this information to design more efficient ways to find objects underwater. By learning how dolphins swim so fast and dive so deep, the Navy has also improved the speed of their ships and submarines. But that's not all! The U.S. Navy instituted training programs for dolphins in which they learned to assist human divers and also perform search and retrieval efforts.

The first exercise conducted with a live dolphin through the Navy's Marine Mammal Program was in 1965. A bottlenose dolphin named Tuffy was trained to repeatedly dive down to the Navy's underwater SEALAB II installation, located more than 650 feet (200 m) deep. Tuffy soon learned to carry mail and tools to the people in the lab. He was also trained to watch over the divers and, if necessary, guide them to safety. Bottlenose dolphins normally spend most of their time at shallower depths, diving no more than 147 feet (44.8 m). But Tuffy

A DIVER WORKS WITH TUFFY, A U.S. NAVY–TRAINED DOLPHIN, UNDERWATER.

THE U.S. NAVY INSTITUTED TRAINING PROGRAMS FOR DOLPHINS IN WHICH THEY LEARNED TO PERFORM SEARCH AND RETRIEVAL EFFORTS.

A TRAINED DOLPHIN HELPS THE MILITARY IN ONE OF THEIR EXERCISES.

INTO THE WAR

THE U.S. NAVY HAS USED DOLPHINS to aid their ships and divers during wartime. During the Vietnam War, five dolphins were sent to Cam Ranh Bay to patrol the waters offshore. They were to keep enemy swimmers from approaching the Navy ships stationed there. The dolphins did this by nudging the swimmers with their beaks. The dolphins were also taught to do underwater surveillance to watch out for any foreign object, such as mines being planted.

Dolphins were later sent to the Persian Gulf during the late 1980s to help out during the Iran-Iraq War. They were used for underwater surveillance, protection, and to escort Kuwait oil ships safely through the gulf.

DOLPHINS MARK PRACTICE MINES FOR HUMANS.

A MILITARY-TRAINED DOLPHIN TRANSPORTS AND PLACES SURVEILLANCE EQUIPMENT.

THE U.S. NAVY TRAINS DOLPHINS TO DETECT MINES, DELIVER EQUIPMENT, AND LOCATE OBJECTS.

was trained to dive deeper. In fact, he holds the dolphin record for diving to the greatest depths at 984 feet (300 m). That's the same height as the Eiffel Tower in Paris, but of course below the ocean's surface.

After Tuffy's success, more dolphins were added to the program. It expanded to include beluga whales and sea lions. These animals were trained to do many different tasks, including protecting ships from human swimmers who might want to attack the ship, locating and attaching objects to targets, and finding sea mines. The animals were well taken care of, and they were housed at the Navy's research facilities in California and Florida.

The Marine Mammal Program is still active today, but it has many fewer marine animal participants than before. The Navy dolphins and sea lions continue their daily training and participate in a yearly exercise with ships in the Pacific Ocean. The Navy plans to keep using the marine mammals until technology advances enough to replace them. But as one Navy researcher puts it, there is nothing that deters an approaching swimmer as effectively as a 660-pound (300-kg) sea lion bearing down on it. That would be a bit scary, don't you think?

NAVY DOLPHINS AND SEA LIONS HAVE DAILY TRAINING AND PARTICIPATE IN A YEARLY EXERCISE WITH SHIPS IN THE PACIFIC OCEAN.

YOU CAN BE A DOLPHIN RESEARCHER

THINK IT MIGHT BE FUN to learn more about dolphins? Wish you could understand how they think? Act? Talk? Why not become a dolphin researcher? It takes hard work and a lot of patience, but it's a rewarding job and can be tons of fun. First you need to go to college and get a degree in any of the following subjects:

- **BIOLOGY OR ZOOLOGY.** Biology is the study of life and living organisms. Zoology is specifically the study of animals. A marine biologist or zoologist whose specialty is dolphins studies their life history. They deal with beached, sick, or dead dolphins and try to figure out how they got sick or died. They are interested in a dolphin's body, their diets, and how they reproduce.

SCUBA TRAINING IS REQUIRED FOR DOLPHIN RESEARCHERS.

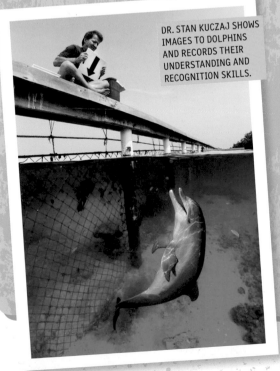

DR. STAN KUCZAJ SHOWS IMAGES TO DOLPHINS AND RECORDS THEIR UNDERSTANDING AND RECOGNITION SKILLS.

- **AUDIOLOGY** is the science that deals with hearing and balance in organisms. Audiologists and acoustical engineers study how dolphins navigate through echolocation.
- **PSYCHOLOGISTS AND PSYCHIATRISTS** want to learn about how the brain works and how an organism thinks. They focus on understanding the benefits and drawbacks of the human-dolphin interaction.
- **EXPERIMENTAL PSYCHOLOGISTS** want to learn how dolphins think and perceive their environment and other marine animals.
- **BEHAVIORAL NEUROSCIENTISTS** study the language of different animals. They want to learn to communicate with dolphins.

Any of these jobs would be a great way to learn more about dolphins and how they fit into our world.

Dangers in the Wild

Not all of the interactions between humans and dolphins are positive ones. Since dolphins and whales are at the top of the ocean food chain, their biggest threat is us. Although humans are becoming more aware of the problem, dolphin species continue to be threatened. In 2006, the baiji, or Yangtze river dolphin, was declared extinct. Dolphins are hunted for food and captured for trade. Because of the regulations placed on many countries, these direct threats occur only in certain areas. An even bigger and more frequent threat is an indirect one called bycatch.

Bycatch is the accidental capture of marine mammals that get tangled in fishing lines or nets. For example, yellowfin tuna and spotted, spinner, and common dolphins all feed on the same type of prey: squid and small fish. While they don't seem to compete for food, or even acknowledge each other, tuna and dolphins are frequently found together. Many fishermen make their living capturing and selling yellowfin tuna to canned tuna factories. Fishermen figured out that if they saw dolphins, tuna were also most likely

SMALL FISH LIKE THIS MAKE GREAT MEALS FOR DOLPHINS.

nearby. They would follow dolphin pods and set their nets. As the tuna swam into the nets, many dolphins and other marine animals got caught as well. The dolphins were pulled underwater by the weight of the nets and drowned.

In the early 1950s, when fishing nets were first used, it is estimated that as many as 35,000 dolphins may have drowned every year. With the passing of the Marine Mammal Protection Act in 1972, U.S. fishing vessels were restricted from causing harm to dolphins in any way. Fishermen started new procedures that slowed a net's closing to allow the dolphins to swim out before they became trapped. That was good news for the dolphins, but not for shark, wahoo, billfish, and endangered sea turtles that may have been caught inside. These animals are simply discarded after the tuna is retrieved.

Nets for tuna are not the only type of netting threats that dolphins face. Gill nets, driftnets, and trawlers also capture unwary dolphins. Gill nets are used primarily in shallow waters near the coast. They are quite large and can span up to two miles (3.2 km) across. They are made of a finely woven nylon designed to snag fish gills. Most fishermen put these nets out at night. That makes them very difficult to see, even for animals that use echolocation. Almost every animal that goes into a gill net does not come out alive.

Driftnets are basically extremely large gill nets. Driftnets are used in the open ocean and can be as big as 40 miles (64 km) across and 40 feet (12 m) deep. Traveling that distance might take you about 35 minutes by car. In other words,

GILL NETS, DRIFTNETS, AND TRAWLERS ALSO CAPTURE UNWARY DOLPHINS.

HUGE NETS CAPTURE DOLPHINS ALONG WITH FISH.

that is a huge area for a giant, open net. Can you imagine how many marine animals can get caught? It's a lot. Some estimate that millions of fish and sea animals are captured every year. Thankfully, driftnets for the most part have been outlawed. The United Nations instituted a voluntary ban on them in 1992, which many nations agreed to follow. Japan and South Korea stopped driftnet fishing completely and even offered to pay the fishermen to buy back their nets. The United States fully supports this ban and has created their own act, called the Magnuson-Stevens Fishery Conservation and Management Reauthorization Act (MSRA) of 2006, which addresses illegal and unreported driftnet use.

Fishing trawlers use a long, open net that they drag behind them. As the trawler moves forward through the water, the net is dragged at the mid-level of the ocean, capturing thousands of fish and other sea creatures. The fishermen

are mostly interested in cod, pollock, sole, and other groundfish, but dolphins, porpoises, and even small whales can get caught in the net, too. What do these trawlers do with all of the fish and other animals they don't want? They just throw them away. In Alaska, where more than 50 of these trawlers still operate, more than 580 million pounds (263 million kg) of dead fish are discarded every year.

Problems With Overfishing

Lack of food is also a huge problem for dolphins and their fellow marine mammals. The sheer number of fish being pulled from the ocean for human consumption, or simply wasted, has a terrible effect on the food web.

Overfishing occurs when the number of fish that are removed from an ecosystem is so high that the fish cannot be replaced through natural reproduction. In other words, if a normal fish

UNLUCKY BYSTANDERS

ONE OF THE MOST SERIOUS ISSUES that Irrawaddy dolphins face is bycatch. Bycatch also happens because of electrofishing or poison fishing in certain areas. Electrofishing is when an electric current is applied to ocean water. The electrical current stuns the fish temporarily, allowing them to be scooped up by fishermen. Dolphins can be stunned at the same time or killed by electrocution. Poison fishing is when cyanide or other types of poison are purposely squirted into the ocean. The poison immobilizes everything in its path and allows fishermen to retrieve the fish and live coral that they want. Dolphins exposed to poison fishing can get very sick and die. Electrofishing and poison fishing are illegal, but these laws are difficult to enforce. Marine officials would have to be present to see this happen, and that's just not possible in the huge ocean.

This is why my diet study is so important. If we can determine the dolphin's habitat, then we can direct fishermen to go to different places to fish. This should reduce the number of dolphins affected by bycatch.

JUSTINE JACKSON-RICKETTS

A YOUNG SHARK IS ACCIDENTALLY CAUGHT DURING A COMMERCIAL FISHING VENTURE.

population can increase by say 5,000 fish per day, and 20,000 fish are removed every day for a week, it would take 28 days to replace that number. If these fish are a food source for the dolphins, the dolphins will have to move to another area to find a new food source. Finding a new habitat is not easy. It must have the correct water temperature, depth, lack of predators, and enough food.

As more dolphin pods are forced to keep moving to find new food, the likelihood of many pods ending up in the same area increases. These pods then have to compete for fish. The weaker dolphins are not able to compete and start to die off. The end result is fewer dolphins and smaller pods. Overfishing is helping contribute to the threat of extinction for some species.

POLAR BEAR ON A MELTING ICE FLOE IN THE ARCTIC OCEAN

Temperatures on the Rise

The warming of the ocean is a concern for our marine mammal friends, too. Climate change due to the increase of carbon dioxide in the atmosphere is making ocean temperatures rise. This rise is also affecting the availability of food in certain areas, which, in turn, makes the dolphins have to expand their habitat areas. Dolphins and whales are able to alter their body temperatures on their own, but scientists are unsure of the extent to which they can adapt to the changing environment. In addition, strange new impacts from climate change are being seen. Polar bears, which previously have never considered dolphins as prey, are now eating them to stay alive. This obviously impacts the dolphin population.

WHAT'S IN AN EXPLORER'S BACKPACK?

WHEN PACKING TO BE ON THE WATER for hours on end, it's important to pack right. When Justine and her team head out to sea, they carry:

GPS DEVICE

DATA SHEETS AND PENCILS

BINOCULARS

WATER BOTTLE

SUN SCREEN
25 SPF

SUNSCREEN

CAMERA

POLARIZED SUNGLASSES

SNACKS

HAT

ENVIRONMENTAL METERS

MUSIC TO PASS THE TIME

PLASTICS ARE A BIG PROBLEM FOR ALL MARINE ANIMALS.

POLLUTION IS HAVING HARMFUL EFFECTS ON THE OCEAN AND ALL MARINE MAMMALS.

OIL SPILLS DESTROY BEACHES AND OCEAN HABITATS.

Pollution Problems

Pollution is also having harmful effects on the ocean and on all marine mammals. Pollution is the introduction of contaminants into a natural environment that results in a negative influence on that environment. In other words, pollution hurts an ecosystem. Pollution can be in the form of actual trash that is found in the ocean, or it can be in the form of chemicals or toxins that are washed into or distributed throughout the ocean.

Garbage comes from people who throw waste off boats or ships or leave it onshore. It also comes from ships that deliberately release it into the ocean. Studies have shown that more than 56 percent of all cetacean species have been known to eat trash. Bottlenose dolphins and some species of whales eat the most garbage. The worst form of garbage for marine mammals is the tiny bits of plastic that float around. Microplastics, such as moisturizer beads found in some body or face washes and in the fabrics of some fleece jackets, get washed out into the ocean. Dolphins can accidentally swallow them. They become lodged in their stomach or intestines, which affects their feeding. Even if dolphins are finding enough food, they may not be able to digest it correctly. There are easy solutions, though. Disposing of garbage responsibly and reducing the number of products containing microplastics you buy can dramatically decrease the amount that ends up in the ocean.

Chemical Pollution

Unfortunately, more than trash ends up in the ocean. The amount of chemical compounds and human-made pollutants found in the ocean is creating issues for its inhabitants. Some of these pollutants include pesticides, herbicides, chemical fertilizers, detergents, oil, sewage, plastics, and other solids. Many of these substances fall to the bottom of the ocean where they are eaten by tiny marine organisms. These organisms are eaten by other animals who are eaten by other animals ... and so on. That means that every animal in the ocean food chain is ingesting these pollutants. As you may have guessed, these substances are not good for the animals and can be toxic at high levels.

The pollution problem affects humans as well. Since we are at the top of the food chain and eat fish and other seafood, those pollutants can end up in our stomachs. In fact, animals higher on the food chain get more pollutants than animals lower on the food chain. This is called bioaccumulation: pollutants ingested from many different kinds of marine organisms build up.

The National Oceanic and Atmospheric Administration (NOAA) estimates that Americans alone eat more than 4.8 billion pounds (2.2 billion kg) of seafood every year. That is about 15.8 pounds (7.2 kg) per person. One would think that the vast ocean could dilute, or water down, the chemicals being dumped into it. But it can't; the amount of chemicals is too great.

Evidence of the danger of

A BRIGHT GREEN ALGAL BLOOM INDICATES WATER POLLUTION.

A GROUP EFFORT

AS SOME DOLPHIN SPECIES, like the river dolphins, are becoming scarce, people are scrambling to help. Efforts to increase awareness of dolphins and whales are ongoing. Laws to protect these marine mammals have been put into place, both for those in the wild and in captivity. Several organizations monitor and give advice on the treatment of marine mammals.

The **INTERNATIONAL WHALING COMMISSION** (IWC) was set up in 1946 to protect and conserve the number of whales on the planet. They oversee and approve the number of whales that can be captured by the whaling industry.

BREACHING HUMPBACK WHALE

The **INTERNATIONAL UNION FOR CONSERVATION OF NATURE (IUCN) SPECIES SURVIVAL COMMISSION** has special projects designed to conserve and protect bottlenose dolphins and other species. One of their interests is to eliminate or drastically reduce bycatch.

A BOTTLENOSE DOLPHIN LEAPS INTO THE AIR.

The **CONVENTION ON INTERNATIONAL TRADE IN ENDANGERED SPECIES OF WILD FAUNA AND FLORA** (CITES) protects all cetaceans in the ocean. They track those that are endangered and strive to keep them thriving by doing research to improve their habitats.

A BRYDE'S WHALE CHASES ITS LUNCH.

The **NATIONAL MARINE FISHERIES SERVICE** (NMFS) is responsible for overseeing and regulating all activities that affect dolphins in the United States. They help with habitat conservation and manage marine resources with respect to dolphins.

WARNING
HELP PROTECT OUR WILDLIFE
DON'T FEED, TOUCH, OR DISTURB
MARINE MAMMALS
IT'S HARMFUL AND ILLEGAL
PERSONS FEEDING, TOUCHING, OR DISTURBING MARINE MAMMALS
IN THE WILD COULD BE SUBJECT TO CIVIL OR CRIMINAL PENALTIES
UNDER PROVISIONS OF THE MARINE MAMMAL PROTECTION ACT
REPORT VIOLATIONS TO THE NMFS ENFORCEMENT HOTLINE: 1-800-853-1964
NATIONAL MARINE FISHERIES SERVICE

HEED LOCAL SIGNS TO KEEP MARINE ANIMALS SAFE.

these pollutants is seen in the increase of algal blooms. An algal bloom is caused by the rapid increase of algae, tiny marine plants, in a certain area. Algae pull oxygen from the water as they grow. Rapid growth causes a huge drop of oxygen levels in the ocean. This affects the other plants and animals living there. If the algal bloom is large enough, it will suck up all of the oxygen, creating a dead zone. Marine animals cannot live in a dead zone. These areas even kill off reefs and other stable organisms. Algal blooms are believed to be caused by the addition of fertilizers, particularly ones with nitrogen, into the ocean. These end up harming not just individual organisms, but the ecosystems themselves.

Tracking Trace Elements

So is it possible to determine what type of pollution a dolphin has been exposed to? Marine biologist Marisa Trego thinks so. She has begun a study with the Conservation Ecology Lab at San Diego State University in California. They are taking blubber samples from short-beaked common dolphins found off the shores of California. Marisa and her team are conducting tests to see what kind of pollutants are in the blubber. Blubber is the outer layer of fat on dolphins. It keeps them warm but also absorbs the chemicals from the water where they swim. By analyzing the chemicals in the blubber, Marisa is hoping to figure out what type of pollutants are in the dolphin habitats as well as the source of the pollution.

Working with scientist Dr. Eunha Hoh, also of San Diego State University, Marisa's team has identified more than 327 different chemical compounds. A few of these are insecticides that are known to be toxic to dolphins. The team continues to work on identifying the other compounds and are creating a database of what they find. Eventually, they hope to figure out each and every compound present in the blubber.

The quest to understand the effect of pollution on dolphins doesn't end there. Marisa and her team are also looking at hormone levels. Hormones are chemicals that are naturally produced by a dolphin. The amount of hormone in blubber can tell a lot about the health of the dolphin. If they can eventually tie the pollutants to the effect of the hormones in the blubber, then they will have some great information.

DOLPHINS CAN ABSORB TRACE AMOUNTS OF OIL FROM THE WATER.

MARISA TREGO, A MARINE BIOLOGIST, TESTS SAMPLES IN A LAB.

YOU Can Help!

If humans are the dolphin's greatest danger, they can also be the dolphin's greatest supporter! There are many things that you can do to help dolphins survive. The best way to combat one of the biggest problems—ocean pollution—is to follow the three R's: Reduce. Reuse. Recycle. Be aware of the amount of garbage you produce. If you can get by using less of something, then do it. Or, if you have to use it, reuse the container. Instead of taking plastic bags from the grocery store every time you go, carry reusable cloth bags. When your parents wash clothes, fill up the washer as high as you can. That way you'll run fewer loads and use less water. Check out the tags on your clothing before putting them in the washer to see if anything contains microplastics. Find detergents that have lower phosphates, as this compound is one of the pollutants that ends up in the ocean.

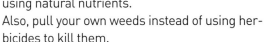

Reduce the amount of fertilizers you use on your plants by creating compost piles and using natural nutrients. Also, pull your own weeds instead of using herbicides to kill them.

Volunteer to help with marine mammal projects in your area. You can do this by checking with your local aquarium or zoo. Support beach cleanup projects or organize your own. Spend time educating yourself and others about dolphins and whales. The more people understand about these amazing creatures, the more likely they are to support them. Never give up. You may be just one person, but you can make a difference in the life of our marine mammal friends!

A SIGN REMINDS PEOPLE TO NOT THROW TRASH INTO THE OCEAN.

ΔΙΑΤΗΡΕΙΤΕ ΤΗΝ ΠΑΡΑΛΙΑ ΚΑΘΑΡΗ
KEEP THE BEACH CLEAN

COMPOST PILES ARE A GREAT WAY TO RECYCLE.

FISH FARMS OFF THE COAST OF FRANCE

ECO-FRIENDLY SEAFOOD

MOST PEOPLE EAT SEAFOOD BECAUSE IT IS TASTY AND HEALTHY.
But are your culinary choices healthy for the ocean environment?
Overfishing of certain species can cause big problems in the ocean.
Accidental catch of turtles and other marine mammals sometimes
happens during commercial fishing ventures. The most eco-friendly,
sustainable seafood comes from fisheries and farms. There the fish
are raised in a controlled aquatic environment. They are harvested
with minimal impact on their populations, and they provide food to sus-
tain many people for a long time. The best part is that these species have
no negative impact on the ocean habitat. Lists of eco-friendly seafood can
be found at many restaurants. Next time you go, be sure to ask for one!

HOMEMADE GRILLED SESAME
TUNA STEAK WITH SOY SAUCE:
AN ECO-FRIENDLY FOOD

DEEP DIVE

BEACH CLEANUP

LIVE NEAR A BEACH AND WANT TO HELP SAVE MARINE ANIMALS? Consider setting up a beach cleanup! Even if you don't live near a beach, you can help out: Look for a beach cleanup to help with when you're on a beach vacation; write emails to friends and family that do live near a beach; and tell everyone you know to remember to pick up their trash.

What you need:

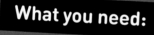

GARBAGE BAGS

SIGN-UP SHEET

SPF 50+
SUNBLOCK

GLOVES

COOLER OF DRINKS

FIRST AID

FIRST AID KIT

Here's what to do:

1. Get some adults to help organize.

2. Pick a location on the beach. You can't cover everything, so make sure the area is not too big.

3. Contact your friends and family to help out.

4. Pick a day and time.

5. Bring your supplies.

6. Tell everyone to be careful and not to pick up anything that looks sharp or dangerous. For that, call an adult.

7. If you encounter any dead marine animals, contact your local fish and wildlife center for help.

FOR MORE DOLPHIN READING, CHECK OUT:

Carney, Elizabeth. *National Geographic Kids Everything Dolphins*. Washington, DC: National Geographic, 2012.

Donohue, Moira Rose. *My Best Friend Is a Dolphin!: And More True Dolphin Stories*. Washington, DC: National Geographic, 2017.

Nicklin, Flip. *Face to Face With Dolphins*. Washington, DC: National Geographic, 2007.

Rizzo, Johnna. *Ocean Animals: Who's Who in the Deep Blue*. Washington, DC: National Geographic, 2016.

Wilsdon, Christina. *Ultimate Oceanpedia*. Washington, DC: National Geographic, 2016.

NATIONAL GEOGRAPHIC PRISTINE SEAS INITIATIVE

Dr. Enric Sala is on a mission to find and protect the last pristine, or untouched, spots in our oceans. Protecting these areas not only keeps them safe, but also helps researchers know what a healthy ocean ecosystem should look like. For more information, visit national geographic.org/projects/pristine-seas

ORCA

SPINNER DOLPHIN

STRIPED DOLPHIN

INDEX

Boldface indicates illustrations.

CREDITS

GI = Getty Images, SS = Shutterstock

COVER (UP), Christian Musat/Alamy Stock Photo; (LE), Andrea Izzotti/GI; (LO RT), Dmitri Ma/SS; (J. Jackson-Ricketts), Eve Edelheit; SPINE, Neirfy/SS; BACK COVER, Norbert Wu/Minden Pictures; 1, Willyam Bradberry/SS; 2-3, Chase Dekker/Wild-Life Images/GI; 4 (LE), Andrea Izzotti/GI; 4 (RT), Robin Chittenden/Minden Pictures; 5 (LE), Chase Dekker Wild-Life Images/GI; 5 (RT), Malcolm Schuyl/FLPA/Minden Pictures; 6 (UP), Eve Edelheit; 6 (LO), Roland Seitre/Minden Pictures; 7 (UP), Lotus_studio/SS; 7 (LO), Eve Edelheit; 8-9, Andrea Izzotti/GI; 10 (UP), Eve Edelheit; 10 (LO), odd-add/SS; 11 (UP LE), Mike Theiss/National Geographic Creative; 11 (UP RT), Francesco Ocello/SS; 11 (LO), Benny Marty/SS; 12, Wild Horizons/UIG via GI; 13 (UP), mauritius images GmbH/Alamy Stock Photo; 13 (LO), IrinaK/SS; 14 (CTR), Stocktrek Images, Inc./Alamy Stock Photo; 14 (LO CTR), The Natural History Museum/Alamy Stock Photo; 14 (LO), Nobumichi Tamura; 15 (UP), Hilary Andrews; 15 (LO), Christian Darkin/Science Source; 16 (UP), Joost van Uffelen/SS; 16 (LO), FineShine/SS; 17 (UP), Andreas Maecker/Alamy Stock Photo; 17 (LO), Jo Crebbin/SS; 18 (UP LE), Morales/GI; 18 (UP RT), Martin Hale/Minden Pictures; 18 (LO), Anirut Krisanakul/SS; 19 (UP), Solvin Zankl /Minden Pictures; 19 (LO), Elise V/SS; 20 (UP), think4photop/SS; 20 (LO), aDam Wildlife/SS; 21 (CTR), Kevin Schafer/GI; 21 (LO), sethakan/GI; 22 (UP), Fotosearch/GI; 22 (CTR LE), Photo Researchers/GI; 22 (CTR RT), Tory Kallman/SS; 22 (LO), Tobias Bernhard/GI; 22-23, NG Maps; 23 (UP), Christian Musat/SS; 23 (CTR LE), robertharding/Alamy Stock Photo; 23 (CTR RT), Volvox Inc/Alamy Stock Photo; 23 (LO), Michael Nolan/GI; 24, Masa Ushioda/SeaPics.com; 25 (UP), Garsya/SS; 25 (LO), Dolphin Research Center, Grassy Key, FL. www.dolphins.org; 26-27, vkilikov/SS; 28, Willyam Bradberry/SS; 29 (UP), Da-ga/SS; 29 (CTR), Stuart Westmorland/GI; 29 (LO), KKulikov/SS; 30 (UP), Dmitri Ma/SS; 30 (CTR), Maxim Krivonos/SS; 30 (LO LE), Lori Epstein/NG Staff; 30 (LO CTR), stanley45/GI; 31, GreenBelka/SS; 32-33, Robin Chittenden/Minden Pictures; 34 (UP), Eve Edelheit; 34 (LO), odd-add/SS; 35 (UP LE), Roland Seitre/Minden Pictures; 35 (UP RT), Francesco Ocello/SS; 35 (LO), Anthony Pierce/Alamy Stock Photo; 36 (LE), Stephen Frink/GI; 36-37 (CTR LO), Kevin Schafer/Minden Pictures; 37 (UP), Michael Seleznev/Alamy Stock Photo; 37 (LO RT), Tom Middleton/SS; 38-39, Norbert Wu/Minden Pictures; 40, Tier Und Naturfotografie J und C Sohns/GI; 41 (A), Tony Campbell/SS; 41 (B), Martens Tom/SS; 41 (C), Mark Caunt/SS; 41 (1), Tory Kallman/SS; 41 (2), SCOTLAND: The Big Picture/Minden Pictures; 41 (3), Tory Kallman/SS; 42 (UP), byvalet/SS; 42 (LO), Dmitri Ma/SS; 43 (UP LE), Vitaly Korovin/SS; 43 (UP RT), mania-room/SS; 43 (LO LE), Daniel Price/Science Source; 43 (LO RT), Pedro Narra/Minden Pictures; 44 (CTR), Uko Gorter; 44 (LO LE), Andrea Izzotti/GI; 44 (LO RT), Alicia Chelini/SS; 45 (CTR), Sarasota Dolphin Research Program/NOAA; 45 (LO LE), Rachel Ceretto/GI; 45 (LO RT), Kwiktor/Dreamstime; 46, muuraa/SS; 47 (UP), Mark Carwardine/Minden Pictures; 47 (LO), Brian J. Skerry/National Geographic Creative; 48 (UP), Claus Lunau/Science Source; 48 (CTR), Geoff Brightling/GI; 49 (UP), Levent Konuk/SS; 49 (LO), Raul Martin/National Geographic Creative; 50 (UP), dpa picture alliance/Alamy Stock Photo; 50 (CTR), imageBROKER/Alamy Stock Photo; 50 (LO), IML Image Group Ltd/Alamy Stock Photo; 51 (UP), Glenn Price/SS; 51 (CTR), Dmytro Pylypenko/SS; 51 (LO LE), Yellow Cat/SS; 51 (LO RT), Lotus_studio/SS; 52 (UP), Yellow Cat/SS; 52 (LO), Tory Kallman/SS; 53 (bottlenose), Pannochka/Dreamstime; 53 (shrimp), Weerachai Khamfu/SS; 53 (mackerel, eel, & herring), Evlakhov Valeriy/SS; 53 (spinner), Flip Nicklin/Minden Pictures; 53 (jellyfish), Jiri Vaclavek/SS; 53 (Hector's), Andreas Maecker/Alamy Stock Photo; 53 (crab), chuyuss/SS; 53 (flounder), Haizhen Du/SS; 53 (orca), Martin Ruegner/GI; 53 (sea lion), Eric Isselée/SS; 53 (shark), Jim Agronick/SS; 54 (UP), Jeff Rotman/GI; 54 (LO), David Jefferson/Alamy Stock Photo; 55 (LE), Gavin Parsons/GI; 55 (RT), Jason Edwards/National Geographic Creative; 56 (UP), Dmitri Ma/SS; 56 (CTR LE), Ingram; 56 (CTR RT), irabel8/SS; 56 (LO), fstop123/GI; 57 (UP), holbox/SS; 57 (CTR LE), Eugenesergeev/Dreamstime; 57 (CTR RT), Emily Frost/SS; 57 (LO), Ken Hurst/SS; 58-59, Chase Dekker Wild-Life Images/GI; 60 (UP), Eve Edelheit; 60 (LO), odd-add/SS; 61 (UP LE), Wild Horizons/UIG via GI; 61 (UP RT), Francesco Ocello/SS; 61 (LO), Jeff Rotman/GI; 62 (LO LE), mikeuk/GI; 62 (LO CTR), Karoline Cullen/SS; 63 (UP), Daniel McCoulloch/Digital Vision; 63 (LO RT), Hiroya Minakuchi/Minden Pictures; 64 (UP), Monika Wieland Shields/SS; 64 (LO), Roland Seitre/Minden Pictures; 65 (UP), Shawn Jackson/Dreamstime; 65 (LO), Danita Delimont; 66, Brian J. Skerry/National Geographic Creative; 67 (UP), Brian J. Skerry/National Geographic Creative; 67 (LO), Daniel McCoulloch/Digital Vision; 68 (UP), Kevin M. McCarthy/SS; 68 (LO), Mitsuaki Iwago/Minden Pictures; 69 (UP), Shane Gross/SS; 69 (LO), Rafel Al Ma'ary/Minden Pictures; 70, Lori Mazzuca; 71 (UP), sad444/GI; 71 (LO), AnaDruga/GI; 72 (CTR), Miguel Rojo/GI; 72 (LO LE), Tim Cuff/Alamy Stock Photo; 72-73 (LO CTR), Marty Melville/AFP/GI; 73 (UP), Photodisc; 73 (LO RT), Pedro Narra/Minden Pictures; 74 (UP), Benny Marty/Alamy Stock Photo; 74 (LO), Feng Yu/SS; 75 (CTR), FabrikaSimf/SS; 75 (LO LE), M. Watson/ARDEA; 75 (LO RT), Eco/UIG/GI; 76 (1), Judy Bellah/GI; 76 (2), Matthew Rakola; 76 (3), Lori Epstein/NG Staff; 76 (4), Zero Creatives/GI; 76 (5), lisafx/GI; 76 (6), imageBROKER/Alamy Stock Photo; 77 (UP), Luca Santilli/SS; 77 (LO), Doug Perrine/Minden Pictures; 78 (UP LE), Visuals Unlimited, Inc./GI; 78 (UP RT), Eco/UIG/GI; 78 (LO), Eco/UIG/GI; 79 (CTR), Brian J. Skerry/National Geographic Creative; 79 (LO), Joel Sartore/National Geographic Creative; 80 (UP), Andy Newman/Florida Keys New Bureau via GI; 80 (LO), Supannee Hickman/SS; 81, Born Free/REX features via AP Photo; 82 (UP), Dmitri Ma/SS; 82 (LO), Zjm7100/Dreamstime; 83 (UP LE), Christophe Cappelli/SS; 83 (UP RT), Georgios Tsichlis/SS; 83 (CTR LE), Brandt Bolding/SS; 83 (CTR RT), Gergana Encheva/SS; 83 (LO LE), ElePhotos/SS; 83 (LO RT), Denis Kabelev/SS; 84-85, Malcolm Schuyl/FLPA/Minden Pictures; 86 (UP), Eve Edelheit; 86 (LO), odd-add/SS; 87 (UP LE), momopixs/SS; 87 (UP RT), Francesco Ocello/SS; 87 (LO), Yvette Cardozo/Alamy Stock Photo; 88, Museums Victoria/Benjamin Healley; 89 (UP), Heidi Pearson/National Geographic Creative; 89 (LO), B.A.E. Inc./Alamy Stock Photo; 90, Courtesy Justine Jackson Ricketts; 91 (LE), Steve Taylor ARPS/Alamy Stock Photo; 91 (RT), Courtesy of Jack Kassewitz; 92 (UP), Brian J. Skerry/National Geographic Creative; 92 (LO), National Archives & Records Administration; 93 (UP), U.S. Navy photo by Mass Communication Specialist 1st Class Bruce Cummins/Released; 93 (LO RT), United States Navy/Barcroft Media/GI; 93 (LO), Brand X; 94 (UP), Louise Murray/Science Source; 94 (CTR), US Navy/Science Source; 94 (LO), Sandy Huffaker/Stringer/GI; 95 (UP), KKG Photo/SS; 95 (LO), Brian J. Skerry/National Geographic Creative; 96 (CTR), Visuals Unlimited, Inc./Louise Murray/GI; 96 (LO), Kletr/SS; 97, Monty Rakusen/GI; 98 (UP LE), Andreas Altenburger/GI; 98 (UP RT), Eve Edelheit; 98 (LO), FloridaStock/SS; 99 (notebook), aopsan/SS; 99 (gps), D_V/SS; 99 (sunscreen), Kraska/SS; 99 (camera), Sashkin/SS; 99 (music), Maximus256/SS; 99 (meter), Rattiya Thongdumhyu/SS; 99 (hat), Anastasios Kandris/SS; 99 (snack), Nattika/SS; 99 (glasses), studiovin/SS; 99 (bottle), pegasusa012/SS; 99 (binoculars), photoDISC; 99 (bag), Pogonici/GI; 100 (UP), João Vianna/GI; 100 (LO), Signature Message/SS; 101 (CTR), William S. Kuta/Alamy Stock Photo; 101 (LO), Vladimirovic/GI; 102 (UP LE), idreamphoto/SS; 102 (UP RT), Tory Kallman/SS; 102 (LO LE), Jordi Chias/naturepl.com/GI; 102 (LO RT), Roi Brooks/Alamy Stock Photo; 103 (LE), Nature/UIG/GI; 103 (RT), Marisa Trego; 104 (UP LE), Image Source/GI; 104 (UP RT), Photodisc; 104 (LO LE), Evan Lorne/SS; 104 (LO RT), Peter Molz/Alamy Stock Photo; 105 (UP), encrier/GI; 105 (LO), Brent Hofacker/SS; 106 (UP), Dmitri Ma/SS; 106 (sunscreen), asiandelight/SS; 106 (cooler), showcake/SS; 106 (gloves), Igorusha/SS; 106 (first aid), Mega Pixel/SS; 106 (bags), photka/SS; 106 (sheet), photastic/SS; 107 (UP), JasonDoiy/GI; 107 (CTR), Klaus Vedfelt/GI; 107 (LO), Arthur Tilley/GI; 108 (LE), Flip Nicklin/Minden Pictures; 108 (LO CTR), Michael Nolan/GI; 108 (RT), Tory Kallman/SS

To Brian, Katie, and Julie: my first aquatic explorers —JS

For the next generation of marine biologists and the families
who support them. And, always, for the dolphins. —JJR

Since 1888, the National Geographic Society has funded more
than 12,000 research, exploration, and preservation projects
around the world. The Society receives funds from National
Geographic Partners, LLC, funded in part by your purchase.
A portion of the proceeds from this book supports this vital work.
To learn more, visit natgeo.com/info.

NATIONAL GEOGRAPHIC and Yellow Border Design are trade-
marks of the National Geographic Society, used under license.

For more information, visit nationalgeographic.com,
call 1-800-647-5463, or write to the following address:
National Geographic Partners
1145 17th Street N.W.
Washington, D.C. 20036-4688 U.S.A.

Visit us online at nationalgeographic.com/books

For librarians and teachers: ngchildrensbooks.org

More for kids from National Geographic: natgeokids.com

For information about special discounts for bulk purchases,
please contact National Geographic Books Special Sales:
specialsales@natgeo.com

For rights or permissions inquiries, please contact National
Geographic Books Subsidiary Rights: bookrights@natgeo.com

Library of Congress Cataloging-in-Publication Data
Names: Swanson, Jennifer, author. | National Geographic
    Society (U.S.)
Title: Absolute expert : dolphins / by Jennifer Swanson.
Other titles: Dolphins
Description: Washington, DC : National Geographic Kids, [2018] |
    Series: Absolute expert | Audience: Ages 9-12. | Audience:
    Grades 4 to 6. | Includes index.
Identifiers: LCCN 2017020448| ISBN 9781426330100 (hardcover) |
    ISBN 9781426330117 (hardcover)
Subjects: LCSH: Dolphins--Juvenile literature.
Classification: LCC QL737.C432 S92 2018 | DDC 599.53/2--dc23
LC record available at https://lccn.loc.gov/2017020448

ACKNOWLEDGMENTS
Many thanks to my editors for their dedication and hard work in
helping me make this book full of dolphin fun! —JS

I am very grateful for the financial support I received both for my
research and to complete graduate school from the Eugene V.
Cota-Robles Fellowship, the National Science Foundation, the
University of California Santa Cruz, the National Geographic
Society, and the Dr. Earl H. Myers and Ethel M. Myers
Oceanographic and Marine Biology Trust. I also owe so much to
my dissertation committee, a group of brilliant, inspiring scien-
tists whose guidance and support proved indispensable during
my graduate studies: Dr. Dan Costa, Dr. Ellen Hines, Dr. Elliott
Hazen, and Dr. Don Croll. I couldn't have done any of this work
without my many collaborators, far and near: Dr. Iliana Ruiz-
Cooley at UCSC, Chalatip Junchompoo of the Thai Department of
Marine and Coastal Resources (DMCR), as well as so many
DMCR employees who helped us in the field, Dr. Louisa
Ponnampalam, Anouk Ilangakoon, Dr. Tara Whitty, Dr. Shannon
Atkinson, Dr. William Walker, Sutep Jaulaong, Dyke Andreasen,
and Colin Carney. I also have to thank my sixth-grade science
teacher, Susan Mitchell, who set me on the path to becoming a
scientist. Finally, but by no means least important, my incredibly
supportive family: my parents, my brother, my husband, and all
of the Jackson and Ricketts clans. I wouldn't be the person I am
without their love and support. —JJR

The authors and publisher also wish to thank the book team:
project editor Shelby Alinsky, editorial assistant Kathryn
Williams, art director Amanda Larsen, photo editors Sarah J.
Mock and Hilary Andrews, and project manager Grace Hill
Smith.

Printed in China
17/RRDS/1